Cesare Pavese Mythographer, Translator, Modernist

A Collection of Studies 70 Years after His Death

Iuri Moscardi
The Graduate Center, CUNY

Series in Literary Studies

VERNON PRESS

www.vernonpress.com

In the Americas:
Vernon Press
1000 N West Street, Suite 1200
Wilmington, Delaware, 19801
United States

In the rest of the world:
Vernon Press
C/Sancti Espiritu 17,
Malaga, 29006
Spain

Series in Literary Studies

Library of Congress Control Number: 2022947701

ISBN: 978-1-64889-865-5

Also available: 978-1-64889-087-1 [Hardback], 978-1-64889-645-3 [PDF, E-Book]

Contents

Introduction

Iuri Moscardi
The Graduate Center, CUNY

2020 was an important date for Cesare Pavese and for those committed to his study: the 70th anniversary of his death. This round anniversary was especially remarkable because it coincided, in Italy, with the end of copyright protection on his books, which were republished with new introductions and critical essays starting from the beginning of 2021 by many presses (among which Einaudi, for which Pavese worked, with managerial responsibilities, up until his death).[1] The anniversary provided an extraordinary excuse to reconsider his human and intellectual character: not only books *by* Pavese appeared,[2] but also

---

[1] Being the publisher already detaining Pavese's copyrights, Einaudi began to republish the entire Pavese catalogue in 2020 and continued through 2021 and 2022: all the books have new covers, designed by Manuele Fior, and new introductions by authors and scholars. These are: N. Lagioia for *Tra donne sole*; T. Scarpa for *Le poesie*; Wu Ming for *La luna e i falò*; D. Di Pietrantonio for *La casa in collina*; D. Starnone for *Il mestiere di vivere*; P. Giordano for *Il diavolo sulle colline*; N. Gardini for *Dialoghi con Leucò* (Torino: Einaudi, 2020). F. Piccolo for *Prima che il gallo canti*; N. Terranova for *Paesi tuoi*; C. Durastanti for *La bella estate*; E. Gioanola for *Feria d'agosto*; L. Nay and G. Zaccaria for *Il compagno* (Torino: Einaudi, 2021). *Il carcere* was published without introduction (Torino: Einaudi, 2022).

[2] Mimesis published Pavese's university thesis, *Interpretazione della poesia di Walt Whitman*, edited and with an introduction by V. Magrelli (Milano: Mimesis, 2020). The writer P. Di Paolo edited for Newton Compton *La luna e i falò*, *La casa in collina*, and two collections of novels (*I capolavori*) and poems (*Poesie. Lavorare stanca, Verrà la morte e avrà i tuoi occhi*) (Roma: Newton Compton, 2021). L. Nay and C. Tavella edited *Prima che il gallo canti*, E. Mattioda *La luna e i falò*, and N. Terranova introduced *Il mestiere di vivere*, published together with *Il taccuino segreto*, edited by S. Renna (Milano: Rizzoli, 2021). *La luna e i falò* has also been adapted as a graphic novel (Latina: Tunué, 2021). S. Ritrovato edited *Dialoghi con Leucò* and S. Scioli *La luna e i falò* (Milano: Feltrinelli, 2021). Adelphi published *Dialoghi con Leucò* with a conversation between the historian C. Ginzburg and G. Boringhieri (Milano, 2021). Aragno published for the first time in a bound volume *Taccuino segreto* (Torino, 2020), edited by F. Belviso, with introductions by A. D'Orsi and L. Mondo (the latter discovered these notes and published them in 1990 on the newspaper *La Stampa*, provoking a scandal among critics because Pavese expressed admiration for Nazis and disdain for Partisans). Finally, Garzanti (Milano, 2021) is publishing Pavese's books in an ongoing new series, enriching them with thorough introductions and exhaustive notes. So far, it has released *Prima che il gallo canti* (edited

books *on* him,[3] including this one. Seventy years is indeed a span of time that allows for the aim of the present collection: deeper reflections about the role and the figure of Pavese as an Italian and European intellectual.

Born in 1908, Pavese became one of the most relevant intellectual figures of the first half of the Twentieth century: he dedicated his entire life to literature, a goal he pursued with tenacity until his very last days. As he wrote in one of the most famous entries of his diary, published as *This Business of Living*: "Literature is a defense against the attacks of life" (Pavese 2017, 117; a note from November 10th, 1938). In Pavese, life and literature were inextricably tied: since all of his attempts at starting a family failed, he had convinced himself that he would never achieve any form of virile ripeness.[4] So, literature became the only pursue in which he found a sense of purpose. Pavese tried to find meaning in and through literature in many ways: he was one of the most versatile intellectuals of the Twentieth century, always seizing opportunities in the most innovative trends of culture and literature. He graduated in Humanities from the University of Turin in 1930 with a thesis on Walt Whitman's poetry, among the first studies on Whitman in Italy, proving an expertise in American literature which was rare even among academics. Then, he began to translate US authors, a pioneering activity that allowed Italian readers to discover masterpieces like Herman Melville's *Moby Dick* (1932); John Dos Passos's *The 42nd Parallel* (1934) and *The Big Money* (1938); John Steinbeck's *Of Mice and Men* (1938); Gertrude Stein's *The Autobiography of Alice B. Toklas* (1938) and *Three Lives* (1940); and William Faulkner's *The Hamlet* (1942). In those same years, he composed the

---

by G. Pedullà, with an afterword by F. Musardo), *La luna e i falò* (edited by M. Schilirò, with an afterword by F. Musardo), and *Il mestiere di vivere* (edited by I. Tassi, with an afterword by A. Carocci), which contains also the juvenile journals *Un viaggio felicissimo* and *Frammenti della mia vita trascorsa*, as well as *Il taccuino segreto*.

[3] Minimum fax republished D. Lajolo's *Il "vizio assurdo"* (Roma, 2020), Pavese's first biography, with an afterword by A. Bajani who interprets Pavese's suicide as a gesture that gave meaning to his life. M. Masoero published *Noi non siamo come i personaggi dei libri* (Alessandria: Edizioni dell'Orso, 2020), the correspondence between Pavese and Nicola Enrichens in 1949-50. R. Gasperina Geroni analyzed Pavese's production in reverse chronological order in *Cesare Pavese controcorrente* (Macerata: Quodlibet, 2020). Finally, the academic journal *Ticontre* has published two issues (13, 2020 and 15, 2021) on the source of Cesare Pavese's literary inspiration between rational and irrational elements.

[4] As a perennial and final admonishment, he chose a verse from Shakespeare's *Macbeth* as the epigraph which opens his last novel, *The Moon and the Bonfires* (1950): "Ripeness is all." This deep connection between life and literature is the reason why many studies focused so extensively on Pavese's suicide, which was considered as the event that could have explained his entire psychology and – consequently – the human reasons behind his conception of life, mirrored in his literary production.

poems of his first collection *Lavorare stanca* (*Hard Labor*, 1936; second, extended edition: 1943), which marked his originality, and his detachment, from the most common poetic styles of his time, like Hermeticism. From 1939, he started writing a series of novels that increased his popularity to the point of making him one of the most prominent writers of his generation. In the meantime, in 1938, Giulio Einaudi had hired him for his press, founded only five years before: Pavese spent the rest of his life working there, holding positions as diverse as translator and editor of translations from English, director and creator of collections, head of the Rome branch of the company, and director.[5] When it seemed that he had finally reached the recognition he deserved, by being awarded the coveted Strega Prize (the most prestigious Italian literary honor) in 1950, Pavese took his own life. Fascinated and tempted by the idea of suicide, as his letters and diary show, his lifeless body was eventually found on August 27th, 1950, in a hotel room in Turin.

In the following decades, this event became one of the most relevant elements on which critics focused their studies on the author. As Brian Moloney wrote,

> most critics have chosen not to regard Pavese as an historian of his own time, and have tended instead to focus more on the Pavese 'case' than on his works, as the titles of their books indicate: *Il vizio assurdo, La maturità impossibile*, and so on. Inevitably, the authors of titles such as these have tended to see Pavese's works as the expression of his unresolved personal problem and failures, which were indeed many and to which his suicide inevitably drew attention. (Moloney 2003, 111)[6]

Pavese has been widely received among English-speaking readers and scholars since the 1950s, as the early translations of his books' show. The decade that opened with his suicide saw the translations of: *The Moon and the Bonfire* (*La luna e i falò*) in 1952 and again in 1953 (with the presentation by the literary

---

[5] As previously mentioned, Einaudi was also the original publisher of all of Pavese's books: only *La spiaggia* (*The Beach*) was published by a different press, Lettere d'Oggi, in 1942.

[6] In this passage, he is referring to some of the most famous essays and studies on Pavese: *Il vizio assurdo* was the first biography of the writer, written by Davide Lajolo and published in Italy in 1960 (English translation: *An Absurd Vice. A Biography of Cesare Pavese*, translated and edited with an introduction by Mario and Mark Pietralunga, New York: New Directions, 1983); *La maturità impossibile. Saggio critico su Cesare Pavese* is an essay written by R. Puletti (Padova: Rebellato, 1961) in which the author chooses the deeply biographical perspective of 'maturità' to analyze the entire Pavese's production.

critic Paolo Milano);[7] *Among Women Only* (*Tra donne sole*) in 1953;[8] *The Devil in the Hills* (*Il diavolo sulle colline*) in 1954;[9] *The Political Prisoner* (*Il carcere*) and *The Beautiful Summer* (*La bella estate*) in 1955;[10] *The House on the Hill* (*La casa in collina*) in 1956;[11] *The Comrade* (*Il compagno*) in 1959.[12] The interest in his work remained constant in the following decades,[13] as showed by R.W. Flint's *The Selected Works of Cesare Pavese*, published in 1968,[14] and, most recently, by Tim Park's new translations of *The Moon and the Bonfires* and *The House on the Hill*.[15] As soon as Pavese's last novel, *The Moon and the Bonfires*, was translated, Frances Frenaye reviewed its 1953 translation on The New York Times (see Frenaye 1953), while Leslie Fiedler wrote, in 1954, the first study of Pavese, a real presentation of him to English-speaking refined readers (see Fiedler 1954). Both Frenaye and Fiedler understood Pavese's literary and intellectual relevance: the former defined him "a young writer more worthy of note than many others tossed up by its post-war vogue" (Frenaye 1953, 4) and the latter cast him as "the writer who moves her [of Italy] newest authors most deeply, who seems to them, indeed, to have defined their newness, their very function" and "the best of recent Italian novelists, though so far less known and honored in our country than Moravia, Vittorini, Berto or Pratolini – in some

---

[7] Translated respectively by L. Sinclair (London: John Lehmann) and, with the more adherent to the Italian title *The Moon and the Bonfires*, by M. Ceconi (New York: Farrar, Straus & Young).

[8] Translated by D. D. Paige; London: Peter Owen.

[9] Translated by D. D. Paige; London: Peter Owen.

[10] Both translated by W. J. Strachan and published in London by Peter Owen.

[11] Translated by W. J. Strachan; London: Peter Owen.

[12] Both this and *The House on the Hill* were translated by W. J. Strachan (London: Peter Owen).

[13] In their introduction to their translation of Pavese's biography written by D. Lajolo, Mario and Mark Pietralunga pointed out: "Since 1960, Pavese has been the subject of interest in many sectors both in America and in England. He is highly regarded in universities even outside the specialization of Italian studies; articles on him have been published in the most varied periodicals, and his poems have consistently appeared in journals and magazines" (Lajolo 1983, 11).

[14] New York: Farrar Straus & Giroux; the book was re-printed by New York Times Review of Books Classics collection in 2001: it contains his translations of *The Beach*, *The House on the Hill*, *Among Women Only*, and *The Devil in the Hills*.

[15] Both published by Penguin Classics in 2021.

quarters even ranked under a sentimental entertainer like Guareschi, the creator of the insufferable Don Camillo[16]" (Fiedler 1954, 536).

Nevertheless, these studies are also emblematic of what has become a typical characteristic of many critics: focusing on selected – sometimes even a single – aspects of Pavese's intellectual and biographical individuality, using them as the perspective through which they put forth their analysis of him and his work.[17] As Dough Thompson wrote, studies and articles on Pavese "continued

---

[16] Elio Vittorini (1908-1966), writer, translator, and consultant, author of the novel *Conversations in Sicily* (1941) and editor of the anthology *Americana* (1941); Giuseppe Berto (1914-1978), writer and screenwriter, author of *Incubus* (1964; transl. William Weaver); Vasco Pratolini (1913-1991), writer; Giovannino Guareschi (1908-1968), Italian journalist, cartoonist and humorist, author of the anti-Communist priest Don Camillo; Alberto Moravia (1907-1990), famous Italian novelist and journalist. It is worth mentioning here that, for Fiedler, Pavese was much more important – as an author – than Moravia, who in 1954 disdainfully defined Pavese on the prestigious newspaper Corriere della Sera as "decadent" ('Pavese decadente', *Corriere della Sera*, 22 December, p. 3).

[17] This is a very synthethic catalogue: I. Calvino's *Pavese: essere e fare* (*L'Europa letteraria*, 5-6, 1960); L. Mondo's *Cesare Pavese* (Milano: Mursia, 1961); R. Puletti's *La maturità impossibile* (Padova: Rebellato, 1961); the monographic issue of the journal *Sigma* with the contributions by L. Mondo, M. Guglielminetti, C. Gorlier, G. L. Beccaria, F. Jesi, S. Pautasso, and G. Barberi Squarotti (1964); D. Fernandez's psychoanalytical approach in *L'échec de Pavese* (Paris: Grasset, 1967); A. Guiducci's *Il mito Pavese* (Firenze: Vallecchi, 1967); G. Venturi's *Pavese* (Firenze: La Nuova Italia, 1969); E. Gioanola's existentialist analysis in *Cesare Pavese. La poetica dell'essere* (Milano: Marzorati, 1971); T. Wlassic's *Pavese falso e vero* (Torino: Centro Studi Piemontesi, 1985), a complete analysis of Pavese' oeuvre; M. Rusi's *Il tempo-dolore: per una fenomenologia della percezione temporale in Cesare Pavese* (Padova: Francisci, 1985) and *Le malvagie analisi. Sulla memoria leopardiana di Cesare Pavese* (Ravenna: Longo, 1988); S. Pautasso's *Cesare Pavese, l'uomo libro. Il mestiere di scrivere come mestiere di vivere* (Milano: Arcipelago, 1991); M. de Las Nieves Muñiz Muñiz's *Introduzione a Pavese* (Roma-Bari: Laterza, 1992); V. Binetti's *Cesare Pavese: una vita imperfetta. La crisi dell'intellettuale nell'Italia del dopoguerra* (Ravenna: Longo, 1998); M. Guglielminetti's *Cesare Pavese romanziere* (Torino: Einaudi, 2000) in Einaudi's complete collection of Pavese's novels; B. Van den Bossche's *'Nulla è veramente accaduto'. Strategie discorsive del mito nell'opera di Cesare Pavese* (Leuven-Firenze: Leuven University Press-Cesati, 2001); Pavese and Poggioli's *«A meeting of minds». Carteggio (1947-1950)*, edited by S. Savioli (Alessandria: Edizioni dell'Orso, 2012); G. C. Ferretti's *L'editore Cesare Pavese* (Torino: Einaudi, 2017), a study of Pavese's relevance as editorial manager at Einaudi; A. Comparini's *La poetica dei Dialoghi con Leucò di Cesare Pavese* (Sesto San Giovanni: Mimesis, 2017), in which the author traces the complete history of the book and proves why it was so relevant for Pavese, whom conveyed all the major themes of his literary production in it; C. Pavese's *L'opera poetica. Testi editi, inediti, traduzioni* (Milano: Mondadori, 2021), edited by A. Sichera and A. Di Silvestro with L. P. Barbarino, C. D'Agata, M. Grasso, M. C. Trovato, and E. Vitale, a monumental collection of Pavese's juvenile poems and poetic translations. Pavese's

to use his writings to underscore particular theses about the failed life and the complex psychology of the man," forgetting that "Pavese's works and not the author's private life were what mattered ultimately." But, Thompson concluded, avoiding this "personalised approach" (Thompson 1982, IX) is the most difficult challenge in attempting a study of Pavese, because the Piedmontese author himself also wrote extensively on his own writing and left us his journal and letters, which were published posthumously in Italian in 1952 and in 1966.[18] He was also, as mentioned before, a versatile intellectual, whose commitment to literature took different forms. For this reason, the best way to look at him, 70 years after his death, cannot be – in my opinion – too narrowly focused: given his intellectual eclecticism, a comprehensive study of Pavese ought to include different approaches devoted to different aspects of his life and his writings. These are the guidelines that I followed while selecting and editing this collection of essays: each of them follows a single path, and the intertwining of all of them builds a more comprehensive representation of Pavese.

A first selection of essays is devoted to the relationship between elements of reality and Pavese's writings, and it includes essays by Salvatore Renna; Maria Concetta Trovato and Antonio Garrasi; and Monica Lanzillotta. In "Cesare

---

biographies are D. Lajolo's *Il vizio assurdo* (Milano: Il Saggiatore, 1960; Roma: Minimum Fax, 2020), considered not very reliable because of the presence of some unverified data; L. Mondo's *Quell'antico ragazzo* (Milano: Rizzoli, 2006; Parma: Guanda, 2021), more objective; English readers can read L. Smith's exhaustive profile *Cesare Pavese and America: Life, Love, and Literature* (Amherst: University of Massachusetts Press, 2012). The new editions of three of Pavese's books by Garzanti (Milano, 2021) are relevant because of their interdisciplinary approach and detailed commentary (introductions and notes are lengthier, in term of pages, than the texts). G. Pedullà focuses on the narratological techniques employed by Pavese as a novelist in *Prima che il gallo canti*. Previous interpretations considered the book as autobiographical: Pedullà frees it from the harsh criticism it received from politically engaged critics, who saw an alter ego of Pavese in the protagonists' political irresolution. I. Tassi analyzes the experimental identity of *Il mestiere di vivere*, Pavese's journal. Instead of focusing on literary models (like G. Leopardi's *Zibaldone*), he defines its experimental nature as both personal outburst and literary manual for his own poetic. M. Schilirò's introduction to *La luna e i falò* follows a thematic approach, navigating a novel built on a series of oppositions: landscape vs story; remaining vs leaving; identity vs knowledge.

[18] Pavese, C. (1952). *Il mestiere di vivere*. Torino: Einaudi; translated by A. E. Murch as *This Business of Living: A Diary, 1935-1950* for British readers (London: Peter Owen, 1961) and as *The Burning Brand: Diaries 1935-1950* for American readers (New York: Walker, 1961). Pavese, C. (1966). *Lettere 1924-1950*. Torino: Einaudi (vol. I, *Lettere 1924-1944*, edited by L. Mondo; vol. II, *Lettere 1945-1950*, edited by I. Calvino); partially translated by A. E. Murch as *Selected Letters, 1924-1950* (London: Peter Owen, 1969).

Pavese and the Landscape of Myth," Renna focuses on Pavese's *Dialogues with Leucò* (1947) to analyze how Pavese expresses some of the most profound meanings of his works through a particular description of physical elements, which makes the book's setting a powerful symbolical element, a literary landscape built upon ancient authors (Hesiod, Virgil, and Ovid). In "'The cats will know': Suggestions for a Representation of a Mythological Animal World in the Works of Cesare Pavese," Trovato and Garrasi rely on Jungian psychology and on cultural anthropology to focus on the symbolic importance of the traditional human-animal dichotomy in Pavese. Many animals are included in Pavese's narratives: Corrado, the protagonist of *The House on the Hill*, has a dog named Belbo; in the poems written in 1950, Pavese mentioned the cats; finally, in *Dialogues with Leucò* the ferine animals embody the contrast between rational and irrational elements. Trovato and Garrasi's is thus an innovative approach to the study of animal representation in Pavese. Finally, in "The «donne vestite per gli occhi» in Cesare Pavese's Creative Production," Lanzillotta re-interprets Pavese's poetic and narrative production, providing a detailed analysis to trace the specific trope of the prostitute. The writer thoroughly depicts this figure in his entire production, since his first poems until his last novel, describing many aspects of her role: from the physical appearance of many prostitutes to the places where they conduct their business. In Pavese's poetics, the figure of the prostitute embodies three main literary themes, all of them crucial in his production and in his psychology: the urban modernity; the alter ego of the Self; and the rite of passage from adolescence to maturity.

A second group of essays focuses on Pavese and translation, and it includes critical analyses by Kim Grego and Mark Pietralunga. In "Cesare Pavese the Americanist Translator: A Chronology of the Myth," Grego draws a complete picture of Pavese's translations. She aims to deconstruct the myth of Pavese as an Americanist, which was perpetuated by critics in the years after his death and crystallized him as a static figure. On the contrary, she analyzes the historical, cultural, and social contexts within which Pavese grew up and how these factors influenced his formation to reach a more objective and nuanced study of him as a translator. For this reason, she emphasizes his translations from Greek and English, considered marginal by the critics because of their experimental character. In "Learning from the Past: Cesare Pavese's First Steps with the American Publishing World," Pietralunga focuses on a more specific time span. He discusses the reception of Pavese's works by the American publishing world in the years 1945-1960. He studies the correspondence related to Pavese's works from publisher Alfred A. Knopf and the papers of the literary agent Sanford J. Greenburger to show how the negotiations and translations from Italian into English raised by publishers and critics may have resulted in limiting a more widespread success of Pavese in the United States.

A third and final group of essays includes the works by Francesco Chianese and Carlo Tirinanzi de Medici: they rely on literary theory and philosophy to provide innovative comparisons between Pavese and other writers or literary movements. In "Recognizing Oneself in a Distorted Mirror: The Irresolvable Transnational Distance and Proximity Between Pavese and Pasolini," Chianese follows in the footsteps of critics such as Ettore Perrella in proposing a reading of Pavese through Lacanian and postcolonial theories. Through these approaches, the author addresses Pavese traumatic encounters with otherness, which inspired his interest in ethnography and anthropology, and the difficulties of a writer in 1930s Italy. According to the essay, Pavese's search for a balance between the pre-capitalist irrational and American consumerism hides a more thorough desire to escape from the radical experience of irrationality represented by Fascism. This contrast is the basis upon which Chianese builds his comparison between Pavese and Pasolini, another author who represented the passage from a pre-industrial to an industrial world in the 1950s and 60s. In "Pavese Between European and American Modernisms," Tirinanzi de Medici deals with one of the most interesting critical discussions among Pavese's scholars, the one regarding his inclusion in the Modernist movement. Despite critics having always considered him as a non-Modernist, Tirinanzi de Medici's analysis of Pavese's works shows peculiar Modernist features (a diffused sense of loneliness, the relevance of psychoanalytical stance on the self) and techniques (the multiplication of points of view, myth as part of the textual structure, conflict among chronological planes), which put them in dialectical relationship with other philosophical and literary traditions, such as Vico's historicism and ethnological studies. From this lens, Pavese's Modernism can be studied in relation to American Modernism, typically associated with authors such as Faulkner, Dos Passos, Steinbeck, and Anderson.

These three groups of essays cover – in innovative ways – different aspects of Pavese's literary production. I found particularly interesting how all of them rely on interdisciplinary approaches. By establishing connections between different Pavese's books or between Pavese and other writers or literary movements, as well as by contextualizing the role that translation played for him, they provide a new representation of Pavese. The conclusions reached by their authors prove indeed the role played by Pavese for the literary culture of his time; more importantly, they show his relevance as a European intellectual, a role that has not been studied very thoroughly so far. I hope that the essays gathered here could serve as a stimulus for new research in this direction, which will emphasize the role of Pavese as a poet, a writer, and an intellectual who always lied at the intersections of different, apparently opposed trends (such as tradition vs modernity; myth vs history; Europe vs America; and so on). And who, despite all the apparent difficulties and contradictions, was always able to reshape them in innovative materials for his own writings and reflections.

Bibliography

Fiedler, L. (1954). "Introducing Cesare Pavese". In *The Kenyon Review*, 16(4), pp. 536-553

Frenaye, F. (1953). "The Traveler Returns". In *The New York Times*, 24 May, Section BR, p. 4

Lajolo, D. (1983). *An Absurd Vice. A Biography of Cesare Pavese*. Translated and edited with an introduction by Mario and Mark Pietralunga. New York: New Directions

Moloney, B. (2003). "Ontology and History in *La luna e i falò*." In Riccobono, R.; Thompson, D. (eds.) *"Onde di questo mare:" Reconsidering Pavese*. Market Harborough (UK): Troubador, pp. 111-120

Pavese, C. (2017). *This Business of Living. Diaries 1935-1950*. London: Routledge

Thompson, D. (1982). *Cesare Pavese. A Study of the Major Novels and Poems*. Cambridge (UK)-New York: Cambridge University Press

Acknowledgments

I would like to spend a few words on the origins of this collection. I originally organized a panel on "Cesare Pavese 70 Years After His Death" for the 2020 AAIS (American Association of Italian Studies) / AATI (American Association of Teachers of Italian) joint conference. After selecting four proposals among the many compelling submissions that I had received, the spread of the Covid-19 pandemic disrupted the plans for the conference, as it did with many other aspects of our individual and collective lives. Thankfully, the editorial board at Vernon Press offered me an opportunity to transform the critical conversation that we envisioned having during our panel into this volume, which, in partial addition to the essays I had originally selected for the AAIS/AATI panel, includes invaluable work by a larger number of scholars. In this way, what was conceived for a specific event can now be read by a broader audience, further benefitting from the multiple perspectives on Pavese offered by the authors: if the medium changed, the purpose of this discussion and the meticulous care which myself and all the authors put into our efforts didn't. For this reason, I want to thank the editorial staff at Vernon Press who patiently and generously followed the development of this collection, always providing support and help through their precise comments and helpful directions. I would also like to thank all the authors for having been so understanding. Despite the difficult moments in which this project was conceived and developed, they always showed professional and personal commitment by submitting their proposal, essays, and revisions in a timely fashion and by being patient. I strongly believe that all their contributions provide new perspectives and directions on the study of Pavese, within and outside the United States. Most importantly, all their essays show the relevance that Pavese still has for them and the modernity of his writings and his work, more than 70 years after his death. This, I believe, is the best legacy a writer could ever leave.

Acknowledgments

I would like to spend a few words on the origins of this collection. I originally organized a panel on "Cesare Pavese 70 Years After His Death" for the 2020 AAIS (American Association of Italian Studies) / AATI (American Association of Teachers of Italian) joint conference. After selecting four proposals among the many compelling submissions that I had received, the spread of the Covid-19 pandemic disrupted the plans for the conference, as it did with many other aspects of our individual and collective lives. Thankfully, the editorial board at Vernon Press offered me an opportunity to transform the critical conversation that we envisioned having during our panel into this volume, which, in partial addition to the essays I had originally selected for the AAIS/AATI panel, includes invaluable work by a larger number of scholars. In this way, what was conceived for a specific event can now be read by a broader audience, further benefitting from the multiple perspectives on Pavese offered by the authors: if the medium changed, the purpose of this discussion and the meticulous care which myself and all the authors put into our efforts didn't. For this reason, I want to thank the editorial staff at Vernon Press who patiently and generously followed the development of this collection, always providing support and help through their precise comments and helpful directions. I would also like to thank all the authors for having been so understanding. Despite the difficult moments in which this project was conceived and developed, they always showed professional and personal commitment by submitting their proposal, essays, and revisions in a timely fashion and by being patient. I strongly believe that all their contributions provide new perspectives and directions on the study of Pavese, within and outside the United States. Most importantly, all their essays show the relevance that Pavese still has for them and the modernity of his writings and his work, more than 70 years after his death. This, I believe, is the best legacy a writer could ever leave.

Chapter 1

Cesare Pavese and the Landscape of Myth

Salvatore Renna

Freie Universität Berlin, Germany

Abstract

The essay dwells on the relationship between myth, literature, and landscape in Cesare Pavese's work and, especially, in his mythical rewriting, *Dialoghi con Leucò*. Moving from the most recent theoretical works on classical reception, it shows how Pavese's mythical landscape is directly influenced by ancient myth and, moreover, how this reinterpretation relies on some specific features of landscape as it appears in ancient mythological narratives. Thus, the paper emphasizes both Pavese's awareness in refashioning the ancient world and argues how his epiphanic and mythical landscape can be interpreted as an example of literary landscape.

Keywords: Myth, Landscape, Pavese, Reception, Epiphany

* * *

1. Introduction

In recent years, scholars have made incredible progresses in the hermeneutics of Cesare Pavese's focus on classical myth, since both Italianists and classicist have deeply investigated what could be considered as a twofold interest. As it is clear even from a quick overview of Pavese's work, his *Arbeit am Mythos*, as Blumenberg (1985) would put it, involves two different aspects: on the one hand, it consists of a theoretical elaboration, which originates in his diary and is later developed in the second part of *Feria d'agosto* (1946) and, later on, in various articles published in different journals after the end of WWII; on the other hand, this interest is realized in a very peculiar form in *Dialoghi con Leucò* (1947), which includes 27 dialogues between heroes and gods of the classical world.[1] Thus, the personal reinterpretation of ancient myth carried out in *Dialoghi* stands out not only as Pavese's particularly beloved work (as he

---

[1] For a detailed and complete analysis see Van den Bossche 2001; Comparini 2017.

himself clearly stresses in Pavese 1966b, 196), but also as the most important and meaningful poetical realization of a close relationship with classical antiquity (which dates back to his high-school years), as it is precisely through this mythical re-writing that Pavese achieves a deeper level of expression.

In this essay, I will take on a specific theme linked both to the theoretical and to the poetical sides of Pavese's elaboration about myth: landscape. In particular, I will first analyse a few theoretical points in which the author emphasizes the importance of landscape in his poetic and how this element explicitly relates to classical myth; secondly, I will focus on two dialogues from *Dialoghi con Leucò* which explicitly thematize the importance of landscape for a true and deep poetical communication (which becomes, therefore, mythical); finally, moving from the most recent works on the relationship between landscape and literature both in the modern and in the classical world, I will discuss if this representation of landscape could be considered as a literary landscape and, moreover, which typical features of landscape in classical myth helped Pavese to develop his own theory of mythical landscape.

My reading moves from the newest critical insights on the author's work. From a broad point of view, my close reading of the two dialogues will idealistically become part of the in-depth analysis of single or multiple dialogues, which have recently shown the complexity of Pavese's active reworking of classical materials.[2] More specifically, the attempt to further problematize landscape and its relation to literary myth will enrich a few significant studies on this topic. Bart Van den Bossche, moving from *Landscape and Memory* (1995) by Simon Schama, stressed how, after the war, Pavese interprets landscape as "the result of an unconscious sedimentation of ontogenetic and mnemonic situations," showing the awareness that "landscape is not only experienced through senses, but [...] it is always formed of different strata of rock and soil, as also of strata of representations and cultural memory" (Van den Bossche 2001, 293). For the critic, Pavese creates what he describes as a "continuous meditation about the metamorphosis of 'nature' into 'landscape', namely the transformation of pure matter into a semiotic artifact, full of cultural memories and sedimented meanings" (Van den Bossche 2001, 293). In addition to this, the combination between real places and Greek mythical counterparts, as it emerges several times from the diary (like in Pavese 2014, 254, 257, 316, 332, 337, 345, 350-351, and 378), illustrates the will to "form and develop a proper mythical setting, rooted [...] in his cultural background, in his perceptive habits, which in their turn emerge

---

[2] See Bazzocchi, 2011; Lanzillotta, 2011, 2014, and 2020; Cavallini, 2014b and 2018; Marchese, 2014; Mirto, 2016 and 2019; Manieri, 2017; Sichera, 2017; Van den Bossche, 2018; Battaglino, 2019; Coppola, 2019; Renna 2020.

from the clash between a certain cultural imagination and the concrete biographical circumstances" (Van den Bossche 2001, 302), while Giusto Traina stressed how Pavese's work is characterized by an aesthetic perception of landscape, that creates a poetic in which "the awareness of the mythical value of landscape itself coexists with a distinct attention towards the realistic side of landscape" (Traina 2014, 26).

Developing these assumptions, in the last section, I will approach the subject from a different point of view, which will constitute a totally new view on the topic. In fact, I will address the question of mythical landscape in relation to the theoretical debate around the connection between literature and landscape and, moving from the work of Michael Jakob, I will show to what extent Pavese's one can be read as a literary landscape. Moreover, I will tackle the question of landscape in ancient Greek myth and I will provide new insight on the author's reading of classical myth by emphasizing how the literary representation of landscape in *Dialoghi con Leucò* is directly linked to some of the most important features of the epiphanic landscape of Greek myth, as it appears distinctly in the work of Pausanias and Hesiod.

2. Santo Stefano Belbo, 1942

In a letter written in 1942 to Fernanda Pivano from Santo Stefano Belbo, the little village of his childhood, Pavese describes an epiphanic episode, that is the moment in which he discovered the need for myth. The finding is fundamental, and it lies at the heart of everything he will write from that moment on. While reading Virgil's *Georgics* among the vineyards, he understands that he needs a literary tool to translate into literature the feeling of what he calls "fantasy of extraordinary power," namely the possibility to express poetically the deepest level of reality, such as "[...] the feeling of being caught up in a fantasy of extraordinary power, as though a complete understanding of them was quickening to life within me. I feel I am an infant again, but an infant, rich in memories of sights and sounds from those early days" (Pavese 1969, 218-219). Not surprisingly, in fact, this realization triggers a revaluation of all he had written before. For him, all of his previous writing, generally considered neo-realistic, makes no sense anymore, since it is not able to literary represent the sensation that he is feeling in this moment. Furthermore, he is also dominated by this new sensation: since his aim is to transform everything into poetry, he understands he does not have the proper language to do that, or, at least, he did not have it until now. That is why, shortly after, he explicitly calls myth into play:

I know my true purpose in life was to express all that in poetry. Not an easy thing to do. My first efforts were feeble, composed on stereotyped patterns, completely failing to reveal the individuality of those trees and this landscape as I knew them. Having gone farther along the road that ends with a leap into the void, I know now that very different words are needed, different echoes from the past, different conceptions of their character. In short, they need to be expressed as myths. (Pavese 1969, 218-219)

In his path towards myth, in which Pavese will write *Dialoghi con Leucò* and further develop this theory on several occasions, landscape appears to be central. The language of myth, in fact, is not only capable of translating the feeling mentioned above, but also of giving life to all those elements of landscape which he sees as the most intimate part of his experience. In other words, he feels himself deeply connected to the places of his childhood and this sensation urges him to find a way to express it. Therefore, myth becomes the only poetical tool able to deprive the landscape of his real factuality and to make it absolute:

Such places, such crags and ravines, trees and vines are as much alive as people are, each with its own personality. They are mythical. That great hill, shaped like a woman's breast, is the very body of the goddess to whom, on St John's night, the traditional bonfires of stubble will rise. [...] The issue is not to remake greek myths, rather to follow their fantastical approach. Now at last I understand the *Georgics*.

Which are beautiful not because they sentimentally describe life in the fields [...], but, rather, because they make the whole countryside rich of mythical secret realities. (Pavese 1969, 218-219)

Mythical communication, as Pavese sees it, constitutes the ability to represent real data, such as parts of the natural world, animated by other presences, which form a sort of second level of reality, deeper and more authentic than the first one. But this formulation, though being quite clear, is a paradox too: if myth is so intimate and so related to the personal landscape of the author, why choosing the Greek myth to express what he felt among *his* hills? How can such a foreign poetical language, so far in time and space, be the right one to poetically render the absoluteness felt in Santo Stefano Belbo? Why the rewriting of mythical stories of ancient Greece emerges as the best way to express a condition so deeply intertwined with Pavese's life, time, and space?

The riddle appears even more unsolvable if we think of how Pavese reacts to the landscape of Calabria. When sent to the south-Italy region by the fascist government between 1935 and 1936, he reads the nature around him from a specific literary point of view (Teti 2011). In fact, while he translates from ancient Greek, he writes that "nothing is more Greek than those abandoned places," and he adds: "tonight, under the red moony rocks, I was thinking of how a great poetry would show the god embodied in this place, with all the allusions and images that such poetry would allow" (Pavese 1966a, 489-490). And yet, regardless of the literary decoding of Calabrian landscape and its deep relation to ancient Greece, he feels that, as a poet, he is not able to render the god incarnated in that place, since it has nothing to do with him: "Why cannot I address the red moony rocks? Because they do not have anything mine but a weak turmoil of landscape, which could never justify poetry. If these rocks were in Piedmont, I would certainly know how to absorb them in an image and give them sense" (Pavese 1966a, 489-490). The nature of the paradox is now clearer. In front of a landscape so linked with Greek myth and explicitly read through Greek literature (Cavallini 2014a), Pavese thinks he cannot render it poetically, since it is not related to his childhood and, therefore, to his deeper self. At the same time, when a few years later he feels the need to literary express his more personal places, he goes back exactly to that Greek myth which seemed to be too different from his own experience. Why is that? The paradox, as I will show in the last paragraph, is just apparent. The key to deciphering it lies in Pavese's own words: "Follow their fantastical approach." In fact, I will argue that the writer chooses to use ancient myth precisely because, as critics have not yet noted, he understands the important relation between myth and landscape, as it particularly emerges in the Greek context. Before coming to this, however, I will focus on *Le muse* and *Gli dèi*, two dialogues which will provide another insight on the topic.

3. Hesiod and men

Throughout *Dialoghi con Leucò*, landscape is a continuously present, as it is influenced by several sources. First, many ethnological texts from which Pavese rewrites some myths are characterized by a strong emphasis on landscape and, especially, on its power to be animated by mythical presences. For example, in *Il lago*, a dialogue between Virbius and Diana, the mythical rework is clearly based on James Frazer's *The Golden Bough* (1890) and, in particular, on his famous description of the surroundings of Nemi, near Rome; in *Le cavalle*, which focuses on Coronide's death by the hand of Apollo, the grid of spatial references relies heavily on two essays by Paula Philippson, such as *Thessalische Mythologie* (1944) and *Untersuchungen über den griechischen Mythos* (1944); in *La belva*, the setting behind the encounter between Selene and Endymion clearly refers to Walter Otto's *Die Götter Griechenlands* (1934). Primary sources are important too. In the most Ovidian dialogues, for instance, metamorphoses appear to be strictly linked to landscape, as it is typical in *Metamorphoses*: in *L'uomo-lupo*, nature emerges as the place in which the result of a metamorphosis can hide, a feature that recalls the Ovidian landscape, described as a "symbol" (Segal 1969), since, as it has been noted, "in the world of *Metamorphoses*, the setting is always potentially more than just a setting: any water, tree or bloom may not only simbolize or memorialize erotic victimhood, but actually embody a victim him-or herself" (Hinds 2002, 134).

In this context, *Le Muse* and *Gli dèi* are of particular significance since they are characterized by a strong meta-poetic meditation. In fact, in these dialogues, Pavese reflects about the meaning of myth and about his mythical rewriting, while he creates an implicit dialogue with his own theory of myth. Through the revisitation of the Hesiodic poetic investiture told in the *Theogony* (and rewritten in *Le Muse*, in which Hesiod dialogues with Mnemosyne, mother of the Muses) and through the dialogue between two contemporary men in *Gli dèi*, the reader is confronted with a thematization of what literature and myth can express. Hence, for this reason, it is remarkably important to analyse the role of landscape within these compositions, since landscape, as it will be shown, lies at the core of this theorization.

As mentioned, in *Le Muse* Hesiod talks with Mnemosyne, who explains to him how to find poetry in everyday life. The poet, who at this moment is just a farmer, admires Mnemosyne's ability to express the real world in an absolute manner, i. e. without the un-poetry that characterizes the life of every common man. But Mnemosyne tells him about a particular kind of epiphanic moment, namely the one in which the world appears deeper and more intense than usual. Consequently, Hesiod feels the need to grasp it and express it, exactly as did Pavese in Santo Stefano Belbo:

HESIOD: It was only an instant, Melete. How could I grasp it?

MNEMOSYNE: Have you ever asked yourself why an instant can suddenly make you happy, happy as a god? You are looking, say, at the olive tree, the olive tree on the path you have taken every day for years, and suddenly there comes a day when the sense of staleness leaves you, and you caress the gnarled trunk with a look, as though you had recognized an old friend, and it spoke to you precisely the one word your heart was hoping for. At times it's the glance of a man passing in the street. Sometimes the rain that drives down for days on end. Or the hoarse cry of a bird. Or a cloud you think you've somewhere seen before. For an instant time stops, and you experience the trivial event as though before and after had no existence. Have you ever asked yourself why this should be?

HESIOD: It's you who say why. That instant has made the event a memory, a model. (Pavese 1965, 158-163)

The passage is dense and important. Through the poetic mask of Hesiod, Pavese emphasizes that poetry can become mythical (and, therefore, universal) when it is able to express a particular feeling. And this feeling, as it is fundamental to stress, is caused by the landscape and deeply intertwined with it. For it is landscape, suddenly seen as removed from his natural state, which is the origin of the feeling of absoluteness. Therefore, the ecstatic moment, that lies at the heart of poetical inspiration, depends on the place in which landscape emerges, and this perception of landscape is in turn the deepest reason for the possibility of mythical poetry, as Pavese had already stressed in *La vigna*, the last part of *Feria d'agosto*:

A valley in the middle of hills, with lawns and trees with different layers and crossed by large clearings, in a morning of September, when a touch of mist makes them fly from the earth, captures your interest because of the manifest feature of sacred place which it had in the past. In the clearings, feasts flowers sacrifices on the edge of the mystery that appear and threat through woodland shadows. There, on the boundary between sky and trunk, the god could appear. Now, I believe that not poetry's feature, but rather mythical fable's one is the consecration of *unique places*, linked to a fact, a gesture, an event. Between various meanings, an absolute sense is given to a place, which becomes isolated in the world. In this way sanctuaries have emerged. In this way childhood places come to mind to everyone; in them have happened things which made them unique, so that they are separated from the rest of the world with this mythical seal. (Pavese 1971, 155)

Gli dèi, which not coincidentally was first titled *I luoghi*, plays a key part in the overall project of *Dialoghi con Leucò*. His uniqueness is marked by different aspects: not only is it the only dialogue between characters who do not belong to the classical world, but it is also the only dialogue carried by two anonymous protagonists and, moreover, it is the only one written in italics. From a poetical point of view, it represents an overall commentary about what preceded it. The two men, in fact, discuss in modern times which was the meaning of myth, why ancient people told those stories and what could be their meaning today. Therefore, it can be read as the continuation of the meta-poetic reflection of *Le Muse*, whose emphasis on the real meaning of poetry is further investigated.

The dialogue is based on a profound conflict: one man is convinced of the poetical power of ancient myth, as he deeply believes in the meaning of these plots and, especially, in their power to be significant even in the modern world.

His partner, instead, is, more sceptical, since he thinks that only empty names and stories have survived from the mythical past, with no ability whatsoever to express modern men's feelings. In this dynamic, landscape constitutes the most important element for the first argument. Since it has not changed from ancient times, it is still possible to tell myths, to believe in them and, most of all, to rely on them for the expression of the most significant human issues. Despite the temporal remoteness, the identity of landscape is presented once again as the root of a deep poetic communication, and it emerges as the only element which can save myth from oblivion:

> - *The mountain is wild, friend. On the rusty grass of last winter there are still patches of snow. It looks like the centaur's robe. These high places are all like this. A few tiny changes, and the countryside becomes exactly what it was when these things happened.*

> - *I wonder if they really saw them.*

> - *Who can say? But surely they did see them. They told their names, and that was all. There lies the whole difference between stories and the truth. [...].*

> - *All it takes is a hill, a peak, a shore. Any lonely place where your eyes lift up and stop at the sky. The incredible relief of things outlined in the air still seizes the heart. For my part I believe that a tree, a rock, profiled against the sky, were gods from the very beginning.* (Pavese 1965, 164-166)

Moreover, it is clear how the final dialogue can be seen as the landing point of a complex reflection about the limits of poetry and its relations with ancient myth. This reflection, which starts in a few diaristic notes, finds a defining moment in Santo Stefano Belbo and continues in different articles through the following years, revolves entirely around landscape and its deep connection both to poetry and to ancient myth. In fact, Pavese decides to move away from more realistic modes of representation, typical of his first works, to fully embrace a poetic of myth which will culminate in *La luna e i falò* (1950). This is possible because of the peculiar way in which he sees the natural world around him, that is to say, because of the personal interpretation of that landscape, which takes him back to rewrite Greek myths. And, right at the end of his rewriting, he offers a final conversation about the meaning of what he has done, reaffirming the deepest core of his conception:

- Who can say why they stopped here? But in every abandoned place, an emptiness, an expectation remains.

- It's the only thing a man could think of, here. These places have names forever. All that remains is the grass and the sky, and yet the breath of the wind is more fragrant to the memory than a storm in the forest. There is neither emptiness nor expectation. What has been exists forever. (Pavese 1965, 164-166)

4. Landscape, literature, and myth

Nevertheless, the matter is far from being resolved. In this section, in fact, I will juxtapose what has previously been noted to some theoretical reflection which will deepen the issue and, in doing so, will provide a new insight. The questions which cannot be eluded appear as simple as profound: what relationship exists between literature and landscape? Can we say Pavese's landscape is a literary one? And, finally, are there any peculiarities of landscape in ancient myth that helped him develop his theory?

In the most recent years, the question of landscape has become one of the most explored by literary critics. Thanks to its multifaceted nature (Marchese 2010; Pagano 2011; Iacoli 2012, 2016a), it has been at the center of what is generally known as "geocriticism" (Tally 2013), which has studied both the dialogue between literature and landscape, especially in Italian literature (Bertone 1999; Collot 2005; Jakob 2005; Fariello 2010; Chirumbolo and Pocci 2013; Iacoli 2016b) and its representation in other media (Iacoli 2008). On the topic of its connection with literature, Michael Jakob proposed a clear definition of what can be interpreted as literary landscape: "If we look at the current state of research, landscape appears to consist neither in a measured and determined nature, nor in the earthly space as something concrete, total or partial, but rather in a visual cut-out made by human beings, i. e. social subjects. To put it better, the landscape is determined by the look of these subjects from a specific point of view; a bordered cut-out, aesthetically judged or perceived, which comes off nature and, at the same time, represents a whole" (Jakob 2005, 39). The crucial point of this definition is the subject, since it is the presence of a subject involved in the literary re-creation of nature, the element that allows to distinguish between a merely ornamental description of nature and a real literary landscape, as Jakob stresses: "Innovative ed meaningful images of nature, such as literary landscapes, emerge only when literary texts refer to subjectivity, only when subjectivity is strongly connected to the text. Therefore, we can speak of literary landscape when, directly or indirectly, the lived experience of nature is characterized by an observer" (Jakob 2005, 40). From this point of view, modernity is totally different from classical antiquity.

For Jakob, in fact, landscape begins to be literary represented only from the Fifteenth century onwards, because, before this period, every representation of landscape seems to lack the aesthetic perception and the strong sense of subjectivity. It is then clear how, to these terms, the question of Pavese's landscape cannot be resolved but in one way: he certainly creates a literary landscape, since his subjectivity is strongly present in shaping it, but this has nothing to do with ancient myth, especially Greek one, which never fully developed a literary perception of landscape. Jakob's formulation is a stimulating starting point, but it does not appear completely ideal for the correlation between ancient and modern literature as it emerges in Pavese's landscape. Since, as Charles Martindale famously stated, "antiquity and modernity, present and past, are always implicated in each other, always in dialogue – to understand either one, you need to think in terms of the other" (Martindale 2006, 5-6), it is necessary to deeper investigate the role of landscape in Greek myth.

At a closer look, the contraposition between modernity and antiquity in terms of literary landscape is quite more nuanced than in Jakob's view. For instance, Ellenistic and Roman societies have recently been described as "unawarely landscaped societies" (Malaspina 2011), i.e., societies that, even though without a full awareness, show a certain aesthetic disposition towards landscape. But if we focus on archaic and classical Greece, which are both the most important periods for classical myth and the most read by Pavese, it is striking to see how different studies have indeed emphasized the strong correlation between landscape and mythical elaboration. Greta Hawes, for example, in the introduction to her recent *Myths on the Map. The Storied Landscape of Ancient Greece* (2017), noted how "stories articulate a particular kind of conceptual map, since the very activity of storytelling has spatial implications: founding narratives furnish a core sense of ethnic identity, heroic genealogies underpin diplomatic kinship, and stories of past hostilities model territorial ambitions and anxieties" (Hawes 2017, 1). Of course, this relationship is formalized in several different modes, but it is undeniable that a long tradition of oral telling contributed to strengthening a fundamental bond between myth and landscape. In fact, since for centuries myths were told in public and open-air performances, landscape became a central part of what was told and, in a way, it even affected the mythical performances (Aloni 1998). In addition to this, the strong religious side of Greek myth constituted another important factor in its connection to landscape, which influenced myth and, at the same time, was symbolically reimagined by myth itself. As Richard Buxton pointed out about myths set in mountainous spaces, "myth, then, reflect. But they also refract, transforming the world by a process of selective emphasis and clarification and exaggeration" (Buxton 1994, 87-88).

This relationship becomes particularly clear in Pausanias' work. The author, a Greek geographer and a pilgrim in roman times, writes his *Description of Greece* both in a naturalistic and antiquarian way (Elsner 1992). The landscape in which he travels is, in fact, constantly read through a mythological lens, for he uses the natural data of landscape to look for ancient myths that happened in those very places (Hutton 2005). In this way, his act of re-telling those myths testifies the complex and layered side of Greek landscape, deeply connected with mythical stories. The way in which the geographer looks at the real world is the same as Pavese's one: every corner, every stone and every tree can hide a mythical presence, in such a way that "geographical space and the narrative medium of myth mesh together to create links across time, across different key episodes which have taken place in the same location and have in turn each enriched that space and made it into a place" (Clarke 2017, 18). This, of course, does not mean that Pavese's view is influenced by Pausanias; rather, it clearly shows that, if both authors are able to mythologically decipher landscape, it is because landscape is profoundly linked to myth. So, while in Calabria, Pavese reads the nature through ancient Greek literature and, later on, feels the presence of myth even in the heels of his childhood, in the same way "Pausania's conjuring up of the passage of gods and heroes through the physical landscape was no more entertainment but a means of presenting Greece's cultural past as a living, still viable present" (Cohen 2001, 95). The differences between the two approaches are nonetheless remarkable: for Pavese, myth is important to express his own most private feelings and what he calls "this experience which is my place in the world" (Pavese 1966a, 639), whereas Pausanias' approach is rather far from this intimate look. However, this juxtaposition becomes critically productive because it exhibits the common reason between the two different readings of landscape. In fact, it is the same traditional connection between mythical narrations and landscape that allows them to symbolically and mythologically read the natural world, which is actually the same of old myth in Pausanias and which, in Pavese, becomes mythical through the mental overlap between the landscape of Piemonte and the Greek one. Obviously, this does not imply that the landscape of Greek myth can be considered as literary *tout court*, at least according to Jakob's definition. The connection between ancient myth and literature represents *one* way (and not the only one) to aesthetically read and re-write the real world, which turns into landscape differently from the more typical way of modernity; a way that, in any case, is understood by Pavese, who is brought towards ancient myth just because he wants to deeply express the feelings triggered by his own landscape and because he is perfectly aware of the relation between ancient stories and their landscape.

5. Conclusion

In conclusion, a number of elements are now more evident. As mentioned, critics had already recognized the centrality of landscape in Pavese's mythical theory and re-writing. However, a problematization of what has here been discussed was still lacking. It was extremely necessary to ponder the exact meaning of literary landscape and to what extent Pavese's complex elaboration could dialogue with some critical tools, as the ones elaborated for the analysis of landscape in literature. Moreover, since Pavese's mythical interest cannot be separated from the ancient world, it was equally important to reflect on which specific features of ancient mythical landscape could have helped Pavese in developing his own theory.

Consequently, from the thesis here developed, it is possible to say that Pavese's landscape is undoubtedly a literary one, since his subjectivity is strongly present in cutting and recreating a portion of reality which is seen through a particular and aesthetic lens. In addition to this, the comparison with the role of landscape in ancient myth confirms from another perspective what the latest studies on Pavese have repeatedly noticed: his reading of the classical world and, in particular, of classical myth is complex, profound and aware of the most important cultural dynamics behind it. For if he chooses myth as the aesthetic lens through which reading landscape, is because his long-time reading of classical literature has made him aware of the deep relation between the two elements. And, given that, the paradox highlighted at the beginning seems to be solved: Pavese uses Greek myth to express his own feelings while being in his own landscape because he perfectly knows what ties myth and landscape, and it is this element, which he calls "their fantastical approach," that he chooses to follow and re-create in his work. Moreover, this is why he chooses to re-write Greek myth, which now emerges as the only poetical language able to translate into literature the centrality of landscape.

From this point of view, the dialogue between Hesiod and Mnemosyne appears even more important, as well as *Gli dèi* can be seen under a new light. In fact, it is no coincidence that *Dialoghi con Leucò* ends with two compositions which thematize the importance of landscape in order to poetically express the absolute, even when centuries have passed since the mythical age. With these two dialogues, in fact, Pavese recreates those epiphanic moments in which men and gods can meet, in which poetry can grasp the absolute hidden under the surface of life and in which, as it has been stressed for Hesiod with words that apply perfectly to Pavese as well, something incredible can happen, but only for a very brief time:

> In a sense, these epiphanic landscapes function a bit like the mirror in *Alice through the Looking Glass*; they function as open spaces that allow

communication and interaction with the 'other', without endangering the permanent disruption of the world order, as the Greeks knew it. Boundaries may be momentarily crossed, transgressions may occur, as result corresponding prices may be paid, but the cosmic equilibrium will be retained at all costs. Mortals encounter and interact with the divine in the epiphanic places, but […] these meeting do not really last for long: soon gods and men find their own place in the world, each way from the other. (Petridou 2015, 197)

Bibliography

Buxton, R. (1994). *Imaginary Greece. The Contexts of Mythology*. Cambridge: Cambridge University Press

Clarke, K. (2017). *Walking through History. Unlocking the Mythical Past*, in Hawes, G. (ed.). *Myths on the Map. The Storied Landscape of Ancient Greece*. Oxford: Oxford University Press, pp. 14-31

Cohen, A. (2001) *Art, Myth, and Travel in the Hellenistic World*, in Alcock, S. E., Cherry, J. F., and Elsner, J. (eds.) *Pausanias. Travel and Memory in Roman Greece*. Oxford: Oxford University Press, pp. 93-126

Hawes, G. (2017). *Of Myth and Maps*, in Hawes, G. (ed.) *Myths on the Map. The Storied Landscape of Ancient Greece*. Oxford: Oxford University Press, pp. 1-13

Hinds, S. (2002). *Landscape and the Aesthetics of Place*, in Hardie, P. (ed.). *The Cambridge Companion to Ovid*. Cambridge: Cambridge University Press, pp. 122-149

Jakob, M. (2005). *Paesaggio e letteratura*. Firenze: Olschki

Martindale, C. (2006). *Thinking through Reception*, in Martindale, C. and Thomas, R. (eds.). *Classics and the Uses of Reception*. Malden: Blackwell, pp. 1-13

Pavese, C. (1965). *Dialogues with Leucò*. London: Peter Owen

⸺ (1966a). *Lettere 1924-1944*. Edited by Lorenzo Mondo. Torino: Einaudi

⸺ (1966b). *Lettere 1945-1950*. Edited by Italo Calvino. Torino: Einaudi

⸺ (1969). *Selected Letters 1924-1950*. London: Peter Owen

⸺ (1971). *Feria d'agosto*. Torino: Einaudi

⸺ (2014). *Il mestiere di vivere*. Edited by Marziano Guglielminetti and Laura Nay. Torino: Einaudi

Petridou, G. (2015). *Divine Epiphany in Greek Literature and Culture*. Oxford: Oxford University Press

Traina, G. (2014). «*Allora la semplice frase "C'era una fonte" commuoverà*». *Paesaggio e memoria dell'antico in Pavese*, in Cavallini, E. (ed.). *La «musa nascosta»: mito e letteratura greca nell'opera di Cesare Pavese*. Bologna: dupress, pp. 25-33

Van Den Bossche, B. (2001). «*Nulla è veramente accaduto*». *Strategie discorsive del mito nell'opera di Cesare Pavese*. Firenze: Cesati

Further Reading

Aloni, A. (1998). *Cantare glorie di eroi. Comunicazione e performance poetica nella Grecia arcaica.* Torino: Scriptorium

Battaglino, G. (2019). "Una palingenesi (volutamente) mancata: l'anti-Orfeo di Pavese ne *L'inconsolabile*, tra demitizzazione e riflessi autobiografici", *Kepos*, 2, pp. 1-21

Bazzocchi, M. A. (2011). "La palude di sangue. Mito e tragedia in Pavese", *Cuadernos de Filología Italiana*, 5-6, pp. 49-60

Bertone, G. (1999). *Lo sguardo escluso. L'idea di paesaggio nella letteratura occidentale.* Novara: Interlinea

Blumenberg, H. (1985). *Work on Myth.* Cambridge: The Mit Press

Cavallini, E. (2014). *«E in primavera le mele»: due frammenti di lirica greca nella traduzione di Cesare Pavese*, in Cavallini, E. (ed.) *La 'musa nascosta': mito e letteratura greca nell'opera di Cesare Pavese.* Bologna: dupress, pp. 101-118

—— (2014b). *«Il desiderio schianta e brucia». Versi di Saffo in* Schiuma d'onda *di Cesare Pavese*, in Catalfamo, A. (ed.). *Pavese, Fenoglio e la dialettica dei tre presenti: quattordicesima Rassegna di saggi internazionali di critica pavesiana.* Catania: C.U.E.C.M., pp. 167-73

—— (2018). "Da Leucade alle Langhe: il «nome della serpe» in Cesare Pavese", *Rivista di cultura classica e medioevale*, 60 (2), pp. 461–70

Chirumbolo, P. and Pocci L. (eds.). (2013). *La rappresentazione del paesaggio nella letteratura e nel cinema dell'Italia contemporanea.* Lewiston: Mellen

Collot, M. (2005). *Paysage et poésie du Romantisme à nos jours.* Paris: Corti

Comparini, A. (2017). *La poetica dei* Dialoghi con Leucò *di Cesare Pavese.* Milano- Udine: Mimesis

Coppola, G. (2019). "Pierre Vidal-Naquet, Cesare Pavese, Paula Philippson, l'età di Crono, l'età degli uomini: alcune riflessioni", *Kepos*, 2, pp. 1-20

Elsner, J. (1992). "Pausanias: A Greek Pilgrim in the Roman World", *Past & Present*, 135, pp. 3-29

Fariello, A. (2010). *Paesaggio e sentimento nella letteratura italiana. Dal Preromanticismo al Decadentismo.* Roma: Bulzoni

Hutton, W. (2005). *Describing Greece. Landscape and Literature in the Periegesis of Pausanias.* Cambridge: Cambridge University Press

Iacoli, G. (2008). *La percezione narrativa dello spazio. Teorie e rappresentazioni contemporanee.* Roma: Carocci

—— (2012). *Paesaggio Passeggio Passages*, in Iacoli, G. (ed.). *Discipline del paesaggio. Un laboratorio per le scienze umane.* Milano-Udine: Mimesis, pp. 59-80

—— (2016a). *A verdi lettere. Idee e stili del paesaggio letterario.* Firenze: Cesati

—— (2016b). *Il verde d'Italia. Orientamenti critici recenti intorno al paesaggio letterario*, in Turi, N. (ed.). *Ecosistemi letterari. Luoghi e paesaggi nella finzione novecentesca.* Firenze: Firenze University Press, pp. 37-53

Lanzillotta, M. (2011). *«Andare per le strade giorno e notte a modo nostro senza mèta». Il mendicante nell'opera di Pavese*, in Lanzillotta, M. (ed.). *Cesare Pavese tra cinema e letteratura.* Soveria Mannelli: Rubbettino, pp. 151-214

—— (2014). «*Molte cose sono mutate sui monti*». *La hybris di Issione nella* Nube *pavesiana*, in Cavallini, E. (ed.). *La "musa nascosta": mito e letteratura greca nell'opera di Cesare Pavese*. Bologna: dupress, pp. 156-83

—— (2020). "Il «fanciullo divino». Ermete nell'opera di Cesare Pavese", *Ticontre*, 13 (2020), pp. 1-18

Malaspina, E. (2011) *Quando il paesaggio non era stato ancora inventato. Descriptiones locorum e teorie del paesaggio da Roma a oggi*, in Tesio, G. and Pennaroli, G. (eds.). *Lo sguardo offeso. Il paesaggio in Italia: storia, geografia, arte, letteratura*. Torino: Centro Studi Piemontesi, pp. 60-85

Manieri, A. (2017). "Le donne del mito nei *Dialoghi con Leucò*: Pavese e le fonti greche", *Quaderni urbinati di cultura classica*, 116 (2), pp. 193–213

Marchese, D. (2010). "Polisemia del paesaggio: dal Romanticismo all'età moderna", *Critica Letteraria*, 38 (2010), pp. 226-37

Marchese, L. (2014). "*I ciechi* di Cesare Pavese tra echi psicanalitici e sincretismo letterario", *Studi Novecenteschi*, 87 (1), pp. 195-215

Mirto, M. S. (2016). "Tradizione mitica e lavoro onirico nei *Dialoghi con Leucò* di Cesare Pavese", *Maia*, 68 (3), pp. 785-808

—— (2019). *Dalla parte di Giasone. Kaschnitz, Seghers, Pavese e la riscrittura del mito*. Pisa: Pisa University Press

Pagano, T. (2011). "Reclaiming Landscape", *Annali d'italianistica*, 29, pp. 401-416

Renna, S. (2020). "Formas mutatas. Ovidio e la *Metamorfosi* nei *Dialoghi con Leucò*", *Ticontre*, 13, pp. 1-32

Segal, C. (1969). *Landscape in Ovid's* Metamorphoses. *A Study in the Transformations of a Literary Symbol*. Wiesbaden: Steiner

Sichera, A. (2017). "Il ritorno del mito, il tempo dell'altro: l'Ulisse di Pavese", *Rivista di letteratura italiana*, 35 (2), pp. 83-96

Tally, R.T. (2013). *Spatiality*. London-New York: Routledge

Teti, V. (2011). *La Calabria di Pavese: mito, realtà, "altrove"*, in Lanzillotta, M. (ed). *Cesare Pavese tra cinema e letteratura*. Soveria Mannelli: Rubbettino, pp. 39-52

Van Den Bossche, B. (2018). *Pavese's Dialogue with Ovid. The Destiny of Metamorphosis in "Dialoghi Con Leucò" (1947)*, in Comparini, A. (ed.). *Ovid's Metamorphoses in Twentieth Century Italian Literature*. Heidelberg: Winter, pp. 199-215

Chapter 2

"The Cats Will Know": Suggestions for a Representation of a Mythological Animal World in the Works of Cesare Pavese

Maria Concetta Trovato
Università degli Studi di Catania, Italy

Antonio Garrasi
Northwestern University, Chicago, Illinois

Abstract

Several textual references witness the presence of animals in Cesare Pavese's works, going from Belbo, the fellow dog of Corrado in *La casa in collina,* to those cats that inhabit his 1950s poems, not to mention the *Dialoghi con Leucò,* where ferine animals often come to embody the contrast between the rational and irrational world. The following contribution aims to shine a spotlight on the peculiar symbolic importance that Pavese recognizes to the traditional dichotomy between human and animal, i.e., between *nature* and *nurture,* while reinterpreting it through his contemporary sensibility. For this reason, it consists of two different parts: the first one starts from a more general reflection which focuses on the archetypical values of the animal image, whereas the second one finds and contextualizes several examples taken from Pavese's main novels, in order to emphasize this traditionally neglected aspect of his literary work.

Keywords: Pavese, myth, animals, Jung, archetype, contemporary age, contemporary literature

* * *

1. Introduction:
"In the beginning was the animal." Brief definition of the investigation field

In the history of Western literature, humans and animals have often been traveling companions and seem to have shared parallel destinies: the innumerable presences that from Greek culture onwards dot our cultural history are declined in numerous and complex variants, polarized between anthropocentrism and ecocentrism.[1] Belonging to the same realm of being, animals are the living beings that remind man of his former relationship with nature, assuming from time to time anthropomorphic, mysterious, or even divine characteristics, not to mention their totemic functions. In fact, the protean figure of the animal manifested in literary memory has acquired, by virtue of the 'similarity in difference', the privileged function of man's *alter ego*.

Due to this simultaneous contiguity and remoteness from the human, the animal world has always represented for literature a precious reservoir of motifs to draw upon for making it a mirror of society. This is especially the case when a given representation of the heterospecific element becomes the bearer of a significant 'otherness', fully capable of erasing the natural boundaries between the two worlds despite the fact that modernity has traditionally been conceived as a turning-around series of binary exclusions. Indeed, in their functioning as a bridge between nature and culture, animals are called to guarantee a biological continuity as much as to reinsert civilized men in the womb of nature.

In the Twentieth century, the human/animal relationship acquires further symbolic and semantic values whose significance often transcends the will of the authors themselves, as it happens in the case of Cesare Pavese. Moreover, the increasing number of studies on Posthumanism in Literature suggests that the human being is usually represented while trespassing or hybridizing with animal/brutal Otherness, especially in his continuous interaction with the realm of Nature.

This same topic of Nature, which branches out into multiple streams and pervades the entire Pavesian oeuvre, is firmly rooted in the idea that "The country is a land of green mysteries for the boy, when he comes in the summer" (Pavese 2016, 10). That is why it should be better understood in its most genuine etymological meaning of giving birth and proving food to its inhabitants.

---

[1] For a further study on "ecocriticism," it is important to see also Iovino 2006, who provides us with the only comprehensive study on ecocriticism available in Italian language.

The starting point of our argument is that his poems and early novels begin in pursuit of the primitive Homeric or Melvillian nature, none of which could be conquered without becoming aware of the pagan and violent elements he had instinctively discovered as a child: not by chance, he finally depicts them as "hostile, not only to civilization, but to his own integrity as an artist and as a man" (Heiney 1971, 366). However, it would not be sufficient, or orthodox, to limit oneself to the easy impressionisms of a certain psychoanalytic criticism, by which the literary and existential parable of the writer has already been investigated close to death.

Therefore, we believe that tracing the contours of a real Pavesian 'bestiary' can be illuminating with respect to various images and recurring motifs in his literary output. Moreover, we intend to investigate and dwell on the peculiar symbolic values that Pavese assigns to the traditional dichotomy between the human and the animal, or between nature and *nurture*, until animals become a metonymic vehicle of nature for the theorization of difference and take on a significant role as carriers of otherness. For this purpose, we will focus on the exemplary cases contained in the *Dialoghi con Leucò* (*Dialogues with Leucò*, 1947), *La casa in collina* (*The House on the Hill*, 1948),[2] and in two of his collections of poems, *Lavorare Stanca* (*Hard Labor*, 1936 and 1943) and *Verrà la morte e avrà i tuoi occhi* (*Death Will Come and Have Your Eyes*, 1951).

2. The face of the other: Pavese's poetry facing the non-human alterity

Although almost antithetical in setting and separated by a chronological span of fifteen years, *Lavorare Stanca* and *Verrà la morte* share examples of the inexhaustible search for the Self that open and close – in a dramatically definitive way – the Pavesian literary experience. Not by chance, in a recent essay, Antonio Sichera underlines how the well-known recovery of the Langhe is based on the two literary personalities on whom Pavese totally relies: Walt Whitman and Herman Melville (not to mention the Chicagoan lawyer Edgar Lee Masters). In their works, the 'Other' is both a paternal and bestial figure, whose experiences push the young poet to come out of the reassuring platonic cave of the known world and undertake his own training path towards modernity. Similarly, in the figure of the cousin chosen by Pavese as protagonist for the incipit poem of the collection (*I mari del Sud*, South Seas), it is possible to recognize some aesthetic traits of Whitman's pioneer and leathery immobility coexisting with the dreamlike elusiveness of Melville's whale. Not

---

[2] Published in 1948 together with *Il carcere* (*The Political Prisoner*, translated by W. J. Strachan, London: Owen, 1955) under the title *Prima che il gallo canti* (*Before the Cock Crows*).

only is he described as a "new Vergil, gigantic, suntanned, and dressed in white" (Trovato and Barbarino 2014, 431-442; authors' translation), but he has also made his fortune by hunting whales on a fishing boat called *The Cetacean*. Furthermore, the putative paternity recognized by Pavese to his cousin through the meaningful sharing of a family silence ("Some ancestor of ours must have been very lonely/-a great man among idiots or a poor fool-/ for teaching his kin all of this silence": Pavese 2016, 4) which, far from inhibiting the possibility of encountering the Other by itself, becomes its constitutive figure.

The word that finally comes to seal the present moment shared by the two interlocutors ("My cousin has spoken tonight": Pavese 2016, 4) is already a poetic one, almost reemerging from an engulfing natural substrate. This is even more stunning if we consider that the existence and the possession of language is what primarily allows the establishment of a relationship between two human beings while at least one of the two finds existential confirmation in the interlocutor.

Language allows men to consider others as themselves and attests to animal otherness. For this reason, the child, like the animal, is the *infans* (literally, "the one who does not speak"). Nevertheless, he keeps within himself the memory of his own experience, which one day will re-emerge. He will then translate it into words and tell about it, which, returning to the etymological nudity of the term, consists in its myth.

There is no doubt that, while renouncing to make explicit the intrinsic problematic nature of Pavese's thought, this *Bildungsroman* (i.e., "novel of formation") in verses, in its attempt to recompose the fracture between the world of childhood and adulthood, had already expressed Pavese's interest for a different and more complex hierarchy of inter and metatextual meanings. These meanings are intrinsically reluctant to the demands of modernity which makes the maternal places of childhood unsuitable for welcoming and satisfying the evolutionary and growth needs of the poet-boy, who ends up hearing the cousin saying: "But the ass, the real horse's ass, was me," he used to say, / "for dreaming up the scheme" (Pavese 1976, 3-5). Here, the animal conceived as a beast (of burden) rises from the beginning to a symbol of the still partially anthropized world, being dichotomously contrasted with the footprints left by the looming of technology. In the same way, the modern world joins the human and shares its industrious silence in a cadenced and inexhaustible succession of cycles and seasons that seems not possible to interrupt. Finally, if in another poem titled *Esterno* (*Outside*) we read "Man is like a beast, and would like to do nothing/It is beasts that can feel the weather, and the boy /felt it in the morning. And there are dogs/that end up/rotten in a ditch" (Pavese 2016, 68), it is also true that one inevitably ends up waiting for work with the same deterministic resignation of a listless flock. The previously mentioned theme of silence turns here into a proper absence of language that sanctions the sudden and unexpected hybridization of the two species and legitimizes, at the same time, the confinement of these places at the time of infancy.

On the contrary, in the already mentioned poem *I Mari del Sud*, the allusion to the subjugation of the escaping whales at the hands of the cousin ("he saw the whales turning and running in a wild froth of blood, / and the boats giving chase, and the great flukes rising and thrashing / out against the harpoons": Pavese 1976, 3-5) culminates in a bloody victory of the human over the feral and turns it into another obligatory stage on the initiatory path towards adulthood[3] that punctuates Pavese's very first book.

3. Among animals, symbols and gods:
Pavese's etho/ethnology and the exemplary case of the *Dialoghi con Leucò*

Lavorare Stanca represents Pavese's first attempt to tell the story of a semi-primitive world where human and animal are two sides of the same coin: animals 'unawareness can be compared to that of children, whereas sudden and painful consciousness belongs to adults.

Later, when his encounter with Jungian psychoanalysis will have taken place through the essential mediation of his beloved Bianca Garufi,[4] he will re-propose the theme of the fracture between childhood and adulthood, moving it from the human and natural plane to the cosmogonic one, and reinterpreting it through the lens of the classical myth.

This cultural approach, free from ideological boundaries, will allow him to insert on the tough strain of myth, with very original results not only in the American narrative of youthful enthusiasm[5], but also the ethical-aesthetic

---

[3] To be more precise, as Barbarino points out, these verses seem to hide a deeper memory of the *Song of Myself* (Barbarino 2019, 61) where Whitman observes "How the fukes splash! / How they contort rapid as lightning, with spasms and spouts of blood!" (Whitman 2017, 189).

[4] At the time of her first meeting with Pavese, Bianca Garufi (1918-2006), a Jungian psychologist to-come, worked as a secretary and translator for the Einaudi. During their brief and unhappy love affair, Pavese would have turned her into his main source of inspiration for the composition of *Dialogues with Leucò* and the posthumous poetic collection *La terra e la morte*. She was also coauthor of the incomplete novel *Fuoco Grande* (*Great Fire*, 1959).

[5] Smith 2012 especially deals with the topic of Pavese's early fascination and later disillusion towards American culture.

conquests of Psychoanalysis (Freudian before, Jungian then), Existentialist Philosophy, and Cultural Anthropology.

As it is well known, these reflections, inaugurated by the early reading (1933) of *The Golden Bough* by James G. Frazer, culminate in the writing of the aforementioned *Dialoghi con Leucò*, where animality often rises to the incarnation of the numinous pre-logical element, represented by the old gods, as opposed to the luminous and rational world of the anthropomorphic gods. Pavese himself provides the clearest explanation of the purpose of the work in the text that would serve as the back cover for its first Italian edition, which can be considered as a programmatic manifesto. He writes:

> Cesare Pavese, whom many people insist on considering a stubborn realist narrator, specialized in the American-Piedmontese countryside and suburbs, reveals a new aspect of his temperament in these *Dialogues*. There is no authentic writer, who does not have his kinks, his whim, his hidden muse, which suddenly lead him to become a hermit. Pavese remembered when he was at school and what he read: he remembered the books he reads every day, the only books he reads. For a moment, he gave up believing that his totem and taboo, his savages, the spirits of the vegetation, the ritual murder, the mythical sphere and the cult of the dead, were useless oddities and wanted to seek in them the secret of something that everyone remembers, everyone admires a little bit rudely and yawns a smile on. So, these *Dialogues* were born. (Pavese 1999, I; authors' translation)

In other words, what attracts Pavese is the persistence of those dark elements (violence, sex, and blood) which make the tribal world the quintessential receptacle of instinctual forces. That is why in the background of the *Dialoghi* we can also recognize the great Freudian myth of *Totem and Taboo*, which goes from the inscription of the human species in the Darwinian continuity of natural evolution, to the nostalgia for that animal dimension that civilized human beings seem to have lost.

Furthermore, the heterogeneity of his studies witnessed not amateurism and superficiality, as reproached by someone, but on the contrary, "a path of theoretical studies often conducted outside the purely aesthetic field" (Borsari 2000, 445; authors' translation). Although the analysis of the links existing between Pavese's works and his ethnological readings allows us to dissect their most hidden meanings, Calvino is not at all wrong in highlighting the particularity of the author's ethnological approach when he states:

This makes Pavese the most different from the ethnological culture [...] he absorbs the fact that the passion for primitive civilizations does not stem from a bookish and theoretical exaltation, nor from a direct participation in the risky problem of certain cultural currents, but from the hinterland of his rural origin. (Pavese1952d, XXX; author's translation)

In addition, we consider it appropriate to reiterate how Pavese gradually distances himself from the irrational mysticism to which the study of the first Levy-Bruhl inevitably refers, and rather addresses the thorny question of the emergence and evolution of human consciousness, from a primitive illogical stage to a stage of awareness of one's heuristic, cognitive, and hermeneutic mechanisms. Conceived in this way, consciousness (platonically) seems to emerge from the encounter with archetypes and symbols, which represent in the first place "the value of image, and this image [...] overlapped to the narrative objectivity. This image was, obscurely, the tale itself" (Pavese 2016, 116). Once this preliminary contact is established, the individual discovers the cosmic reality that transfigures everyday things and gives them the value and meaning without which the world would be impoverished.

Armanda Guiducci asserts that Pavese "always speaks to us of memories in a geological and archaeological sense, as superimposed stratifications, mixed with waste materials and concealing their core at a deeper level. He then speaks of excavation, of deposits, of veins to be found" (Guiducci 1974, 42; authors' translation). Therefore, while Pavese seems to borrow the well-known Freudian theory of *après-coup* according to which the intrinsic meaning of an event must always be attributed in the aftermath, the reference to Jung becomes manifest in the definition of symbol, which, as Freud's former disciple had significantly observed, has to be identified with "the image of a content that for the most part transcends consciousness" (Jung 1965, 87; authors' translation).

Similarly, the reduction to clarity of his own myths – in which Pavese continuously engages himself – is never static or rational, but marked by the reinterpretation of mythological symbols, which still bear the traces of the original chaos. On the contrary, if sex is one of the most important aspects of a sensitive life and, at the same time, the most explicit manifestation of the bloody vitality of the 'savage', it will turn out to be a recurrent feminine *Urbild* throughout the entire period of Pavesian literary production. It is worth mentioning that panic and supernatural dimension always converge in the female figures that will later justify the tragic and heterogeneous classicism of the *Dialoghi con Leucò*. It is also significant that, with the opening dialogue of the collection entitled *La nube* (*The Cloud*), Pavese places us immediately on the threshold of a putrefied titanic world and underlines its constitutive hybridity, observing that in it "very different creatures were still permitted to mate and interbreed" (Pavese 1965, 2). In the introduction to the dialogue, he puts forward the hypothesis that the inhabitants of the titanic world might share the same blood of the heroes.

On the same topic of hybridizations, the introductory note to the dialogue *Le cavalle* (*The Mares*), dated on the manuscript February 25th-26th, 1947, places the reader at the gates of a hypogeum inhabited by a "swarm of monsters" (Pavese 1965, 2) in which animal symbolism abounds. This is the mythologem constituting the background to the birth of Asclepius, God of medicine and snakes, whom Hermes Psychopomp – in turn, emerged from a protean fluidity[6] hastens to eviscerate from the burning body of his mother Coronides. He later will entrust him to none other than the care of the centaur Chiron, an ontologically liminal figure, half-man and half-horse. In reality, the death of Coronides constitutes the true hermeneutic nucleus of this dialogue because the Princess of the Lapiths, in her double semblance of woman and of mare, seems to keep within herself the trace of the bestial origin that had generated her. It is also worth mentioning that the destruction of her female body on the above-mentioned bonfire resembles a sort of propitiatory rite, as much as the erasure of female maternity and its re-inscription as the territory of men maintains that fantasy of male self-generation that we have been discussing about in the previous pages of this essay as a distinctive trait of Pavese's literary output.

Paula Philipsson, whose *Tessalysche Mythologie* represents one of the major sources for the composition of the dialogue that we are analyzing, states that the Hellenic gods are neither human nor animalistic. Nevertheless, the human figure and the animal figure are forms of epiphany, in which those divinities made themselves known in that form of knowledge – and approximation to metaphysics – which is myth. Similarly, Mario Untersteiner in his *La fisiologia del mito*, another of the sources consulted by Pavese, underlines how, by a sort of metaphysical imperative, the divinity was forced to ignore the boundaries between the various kingdoms of nature. Therefore, appearing in anthropomorphic or theriomorphic, phytomorphic or mixed aspect, the divinity succeeds in representing the substantial unity of nature through metamorphoses that do not change the divine entity.

As approximate as we may consider it in the light of the most recent ethno-anthropological studies, the thesis supported by Untersteiner is not entirely inappropriate. According to him, primitives, like children and animals, cannot

---

[6] CHIRON: What do you expect? We are animals. And even you, Lord of the Ways, at Larissa you were once bull's sperm. And in those early days you mated in the slime with all the shapeless things of blood. You, Hermes, should understand. (Pavese 1965, 22).

distinguish between thought and being. Therefore, the thought aroused by the representation of a god is identified with the presence of the god itself. Later, the animistic representation of the divine would once again reach its first concrete configuration and its intimate wholeness through language. When this sort of image enters the clear light of language, it takes on a more defined meaning.

If we then think that the common Chthonian origin confers both Hermes and Asclepius the attribute of the serpent coiled around a rod, it will not surprise us to discover that Asclepius, long before becoming the son of Apollo and the professional god of doctors, had been a great Chthonian god of Thessaly. The god himself is representative of a pantheistic world, where long before the advent of Zeus every natural element, from minerals to plants, passing through the animal kingdom, ended up being permeated by divinity.

The same need for significance would have been answered first by the inexhaustible creativity of the Greek writers: the happy pen of the epic poet. In fact, starting from the so-called theogonies and cosmogonies, we would finally arrive, through a tortuous intellectual path, to a word that celebrates the individual and collective enterprises of warriors partially transfigured into heroes, a shining example of moral rectitude and self-denial.

It is worth mentioning here that the drafting of *Le cavalle* had been significantly preceded by that of *L'Ospite* (*The Guest*), where the demigod Heracles assumes the role of a civilizing hero, victoriously opposing the karst gynocratic brutality of Litierses and its sacrificial rites to the Mother Earth, whose continuous voracity refers to the primeval animality.

Again, according to the myth taken up by Pavese in *La madre* (*The Mother*), it was the inequitable partition of a boar that caused Meleager's violent death at the hands of his uncle. Pavese had gone even further by identifying the signifier in the skin of the sacrificed animal, otherwise known as the material seal of the pact of love and hunt that Meleager had made with his partner Atalanta, making her say: "The boarskin will lie on our marriage-bed. It will be like your blood-price —yours and mine" (Pavese 1965, 50).

The motif of the sacrificial brutality returns with arrogance in *L'uomo-lupo* (*The Werewolf*) that traces the bloody events linked to the death of Lycaon, lord of Arcady. Here, the insistence on the feral traits assumed by the old monarch in the words of the First Hunter ("Had the heart of an animal as well as the hide. It's been a long time since a wolf that size has been seen in these woods") seems to mitigate the gravity of the crime committed ("It's not the first time an animal's been killed"), while almost justifying it. ("That's not our worry. The dogs flushed him. It's none of our business who he was": Pavese 1965, 77). In other words, in the figure of the agonizing Lycaon, symbol of a degraded humanity to be constantly monitored and punished, dehumanization alternates brutality ("It isn't a corpse, it's a carcass,": Pavese, 1965, 77; and beyond: "the last thing he saw was men hunting him down. Do you think it matters to him whether he rots underground, like a man?": Pavese, 1965, 80) and silent longing for *pietas*, whose values are embodied in the words uttered by the Second Hunter ("But when he died and looked at us, he knew he was a man. His eyes said he was": Pavese 1965, 80) in the extreme moment of Lycaon's passing away.

To conclude this series of considerations, we would like to underline how the approach of the human to the animal often derives, in Pavese, from the awareness of the fall to the loss of a presumed original integrity. In the dialogue *Gli uomini*, the human condition is mercilessly compared to that of poor worms, a rhetorical device behind which Pavese hides the reference to another *topos* of the classical world, i.e., the well-known φθόνος τῶν θεῶν, the envy of the gods. This should be better reinterpreted in the light of a Twentieth-century sensitivity that makes it no longer "the malevolent aversion to the momentary happiness of a mortal, but a poignant gaze towards a misery that – paradoxically – attracts and conquers" (Sichera 2015, 302; authors' translation). Envied by Circe, who would literally like turn him into a pig or a wolf, is Odysseus. In fact, it is precisely by refusing the bestial metamorphosis that culminates in a brutal embrace ("I amuse myself with them, Leucò, as best I can. [...] All the others turn into animals at my touch; they go crazy and come after me, like wild beasts [...] But with them I mustn't even smile. I feel them mount me and then run off back to their lairs": Pavese 1965, 111) that the Homeric hero succeeds in instilling in the ancient Mediterranean divinity the desire to be ontologically similar to him, until playing the same role that had belonged to mortal Penelope.

Unlike their male counterpart, who often remains victim of so much proximity, in the female figures that inhabit the *Dialoghi* the contiguity to the animal kingdom often combines the usual ruthlessness with a latent sensual trait. This is precisely the case of Artemis in *La belva (The Beast)*, dialogue in which Pavese infuses an obvious autobiographical component. She represents a clear classical hypostasis of the pre-Hellenic Πότνια Θηρῶν, (i.e., "The Mistress of Beasts") who came to disturb, with her celestial and nightmarish presence, the sleep of her ancient companion Endymion, the Aeolian shepherd and prince. It appears clear from the beginning that the insistence on the physical features of the goddess pursues a dual purpose. In fact, if, on the one hand, the writer makes use of a manifest antiphrastic procedure aimed at emphasizing the disconcerting extent of the power hiding inside an apparently minute body, on the other hand, it highlights the proximity of the virgin goddess to the kingdom of Nature. Here, the two polar and primeval forces of

Eros and Thanatos dominate uncontested with their hints of coitus (the "foia" of which we read several times in the manuscript of the aforementioned *L'uomo-lupo*) and death.

Therefore, if indeterminacy is one of the attributes of the divine, then it should not be surprising that the semantic and rhythmic structure of a dialogue like *La belva* revolves around the two sensory verbs *par excellence*, namely *to look* and *to touch*: "I never touch her hand," (Pavese 1965, 36) as a dreamy Endymion confesses to the Stranger. A more than physical incommunicability, which Walt Whitman would have put in such prophetic words:

> Each man to himself and each woman to herself, is the word of the past and present, and
> the true [word of immortality;
> No one can acquire for another – not one,
> Not one can grow for another – not one. (Whitman 2017, 518)

Later, Artemis herself, *Urbild* of the lunar virgin, is the one to whom "no one has ever touched [the] knee" (Pavese 1965, 38). Likewise, her touch is like the rough caress one would give to a dog or to the trunk of a tree. In some way, the words that Endymion uses to describe his nocturnal encounter with Artemis are all attributable to the natural and animal world, which the goddess dominates and from which she comes. Just consider, by way of example, the comparison between her nature, and that "of a she-wolf, a doe, or a snake" (Pavese 1965, 34) in a kind of ascendant climax, which emphasizes the urgency and drama of sexual desire. Finally, there are numerous and repeated references to the sensorial semantic of sight: one for all, that "I saw her looking at me, looking at me" (Pavese 1965, 35), preluding to an encounter in which the dominant trait of the shepherd's possession by the goddess becomes, at the same time, physical and mental. Endymion himself provides the clearest textual indication of his own annihilation, when he confesses that he would like to "let me spill my blood on the ground at her feet, my flesh torn by her hounds" (Pavese 1965, 37).

This brings us to another of the themes dear to Pavese, namely the assumption of the female body as an integral and, indeed, constitutive part of a natural and precultural world. The Feminist Australian philosopher Elisabeth Grosz significantly states that

> the male/female opposition has been closely allied with the mind/body opposition. Typically, femininity is represented (either explicitly or implicitly) in one of two ways in this cross- pairing of oppositions: either mind is rendered equivalent to the masculine and the body equivalent

to the feminine (thus ruling out woman a priori as possible subjects of knowledge, or philosophers) or each sex is attributed its own form of corporeality. (Grosz 1994, 14)

Pavese's women are often immersed in a natural world that ends up becoming a part of their own body: many examples of the equivalence between women and animals can be found in his poetry. Think of *Il dio caprone* (1933), where women figure as goats, or *L'istinto* (1936), in which they are depicted as the sexual object of an old man and compared to dogs in this way: "The old man remembers how once, in full daylight, / he did it in a wheatfield, just like a dog. / Who the bitch was, he can't remember; he remembers the hot sun / and the sweat, and wanting to keep on going forever" (Pavese 1976, 92).

Last but not least, in the dialogue *Il toro* (*The Bull*), "the big blond women" who usually spend their time lying in the sun on the terraces of the palace, ripen as if they were fruits choosing not to respond to any other law than the one imposed by their biological rhythm, while Ariadne, whom Theseus knew carnally under the appearance of a bull, is beautiful because she is "made of earth and sun" (Pavese 1965, 119).

It appears clear that the female body too is "a stand-in for the natural world – zoological, botanical, and geological – whose instincts, ripening, heat, and colors are available for manipulation and exploitation by men, except in those instances when its propitiation has been insufficiently or improperly enacted". On the other hand, it is undeniable that Pavese's works always "sustain the alterity of women and nature with respect to men, [...] on which the (male) subject of modernity is founded" (Leake 2014, 40). To put it in other words, even Pavese's characters show speciesist attitudes, where speciesism is akin to "sexism or racism in privileging humans, males, and whites over all others" (Braidotti 2011, 90). Secondly, if in *Lavorare Stanca* the woman's body had already been inextricably connected to the natural cycle of coitus, generation, and death, almost exhausting its function in this preponderant biological component, in *Dialoghi con Leucó* the animal-woman and the woman-animal are "two sides of the same fracture that cannot be bridged either on one side or the other" (Salvadori 2017, 46; authors' translation). *Lavorare stanca* provides us, for instance, with the exemplary case of *Una stagione* (*A Season*), where "once this woman's body was all firm, young / flesh [w]hen she was carrying a child," but "with time and feeding all those / other bodies with her own, even she was broken. / She's nothing to look at now, all her strength gone" (Pavese 1976, 65). The above-mentioned contrast is, therefore, never resolved in favor of one or the other ethical-aesthetic component. Nevertheless, as we will see later, the hybridization that plays such a large part in the connective tissue and semantic economy of a work such as the *Dialoghi* is certainly not the only symbolic procedure through which the animal world finds space in Pavese's work.

4. "Before the rooster crows, you will disown me three times": what animals mean in Pavese's last works

In *The House on the Hill*, the protagonist, Corrado, a former Science professor who finds shelter from the rage of the Second World War in the home of two elderly women, strenuously defends his decision to devote himself to solitude and the painful contemplation of what is happening around him, wrapping himself in his existential cocoon. Only Belbo, the big dog of the owners, can enter it. Moreover, it is not surprising that, for his name, Pavese chooses a name intimately connected with the maternal places of childhood and memory: the small river passing through his native town of Santo Stefano Belbo, named after it. Davide Lajolo, one of Pavese's friends and his first biographer, had already argued that it was of fundamental critical importance to investigate that rural dimension for the formation of the author.

According to him,

> not only in order to know him as a boy [...] but also because those sentiments, those visions, that reality and those dreams characterized his life and his art. Even the myths, literary or not, that would later pursue him and carry him far from reality in the difficult search for truth must be linked to the fables and myths of which he was deeply fond as a child. (Lajolo 1983, 4)

It will be equally significant to hear Anguilla (Eel), the central and distinctly autobiographical figure of *The Moon and the Bonfires*, saying: "Your own village means that you are not alone, that you know there's something of you in the people and the plants and the soil, that even when you are not there it waits to welcome you" (Pavese 1952b, 6).

This is particularly important to be found in Pavese's book that, deepening more than any others the themes of removal and subsequent return to the homeland, configures itself as the final fulfillment of a precise ethical and aesthetic mandate. Pavese himself, although totally accustomed to the life of the Turin metropolis, to which an equally visceral transport binds him, had soon experienced to what extent the Langa gradually changes into a land awaiting and saying no words, unaware of having given birth to one of its last, passionate, and prolific writers.

The silence pairs with fidelity and waiting. For the Pavesian exiles, the Langa takes on not only the well-known and explored maternal connotations, but also arouses a visceral and instinctive feeling of maternal belonging, which, in Anguilla's case, seems to contradict the 'slipperiness' suggested by his name.

Returning now to Corrado, the memory and perhaps the typically infantile desire to accompany a dog during his raids in the woods ("Ever since childhood it has seemed to me that to go through the woods without a dog is to miss a large share of life and the earth's secrets" (Pavese 1956, 6)), emerge since the initial pages of the novel. Furthermore, beyond he confesses: "'You won't believe it', I said to Cate. 'But this dog is my sole companion'" (Pavese 1956, 33). This is a way of escaping from the 'maternal prison', which is, for him, the house on the hills, where he lives as both a guest and a prisoner. Corrado often remains in a long and frequent silence which, far from being the preparatory and fruitful silence to which Pavese referred in his diary *Il Mestiere di vivere (This Business of Living)* writing: "What is to come will emerge only after long suffering, long silence" (Pavese 2009, 26) translates into something more than sentimental aphasia. For a similar reason, the encounter with a mouse with strongly anthropized traits in the aftermath of the bombings in Turin opens one of the central chapters of *La casa* and makes the protagonist fully aware of his own precariousness and fear, already experienced on the physical level: "When winter came, it was *I* who became afraid" (Pavese 1956, 110; italics in the text).

More than the bitter cold, to which he says he is accustomed (like mice and everyone), it disturbs him to feel in his body the effects of a subtle neurosis that pushes him to assume the same cautious and throbbing attitude of a frightened hare. It is important to underline that his overt attempt to 'become an animal', namely zoomimesis, has not to be taken here as mere imitation or identification with the animal, but as an "alliance with the anomalous" (Vignola 2013, 122).

Later, Corrado confesses that he is envious of the beasts and their apparent unawareness and lack of communication: "I would like to have skulked off, like a rat. Animals, I reflected, did not know what was going to happen. I envied them" (Pavese 1956, 111). It is a classical and canonized topic but rewritten and changed, given that it is no longer looked at from a monolithic distance, but as the unsuccessful outcome of a harrowing hand-to-hand battle with the unspeakable. Consequently, while Corrado's 'illness' is caused by the wholly Dostoevskian hypertrophy of a paralyzing thought, the two landladies are strong in their bestial unawareness, and oppose the winds of war with a solidity that makes the return to the warmth of that den almost indispensable. It is therefore not surprising that the caretaker of the ivory tower where Corrado almost undergoes a confinement illusorily masked with freshly washed laundry and home-made food, is no longer a very young lady, Elvira, from whose sentimental claims the protagonist evades with the same urgency of a hunted animal. Incredibly, however, the dog Belbo legitimizes the univocal claim of emotional proximity between the two characters ("'[Elvira] is your dog's mother', she said quietly. 'Doesn't she expect you to give an account of where you've been all day?'": Pavese 1956, 47). In the same perspective, it is relevant to note that Corrado's first contact with his former lover Cate takes place in the darkness of a late evening, allowing them to talk to each other as if in a mask.

They stage an early skirmish with semi-serious tones with plenty of references to the classical theme of man-hunter and woman-prey ("'You're not going to eat me, are you?' she threw at me": Pavese 1956, 17), in an instinctual outpouring that anticipates, for the protagonist, the rational moment of acknowledgment, or rather of the belated and hesitant recognition, of the woman.

On the other hand, Corrado's memories convey an "enduring anxiety about the female body made emergent and operative in the equation between women and (wild) animals in several of his novels as well as throughout Pavese's poetic oeuvre" (Leake 2014, 39): there, lovemaking is often awkward, like a fight. "'What difference is there', I used to say to her, 'between scrapping round and having a bit of a cuddle?' So, on one or two occasions we lay on the grass in a half-hearted way" (Pavese 1956, 20), and no words are needed ("We did not waste time talking and that gave me courage": Pavese 1956, 20). Especially if compared with Anna Maria, an elegant, rich and cultivated woman from Corrado's past who is mentioned *in absentia*, that is while she is no longer there, Cate's personality is defined by some 'bestial' traits: silence, clumsiness, and loyalty, to mention just a few. This partially justifies the rashness of the protagonist's early affair with her: "'You made love to me', she added quietly. 'And you didn't care a damn about me'" (Pavese 1956, 51) is one of her first statements in the novel to prove Corrado wrong.

Most importantly, since the beginning of the novel, we realize that Corrado contrasts his restless wandering as a cynic, capable only of being pleased with his own radical loneliness and not remedying it, to the vital immediacy of his dog, whose dynamism is all resolved in the inexhaustible exploration of the woods that surround the house ("It is pleasant to walk among the hills with a dog; as one goes along, he noses out roots, holes, ravines, undivined existences, thereby increasing for us the pleasure of discovery": Pavese 1956, 10).

Indeed, the closing pages of the novel will only confirm the solipsistic choice of the character, although a subtle form of regret is still reserved only for the memory of the ancient companion of forest raids ("I am sorry that Belbo was left behind in Turin": Pavese 1956, 195). On the other hand, the 'maternal' attitude Corrado shows towards Cate's son, Dino, while assessing their undeniable resemblance, recalls that of any wild animal carrying its cubs by the scruff in order to protect them.

Silent and conscious witnesses of an impenetrable loneliness in which there is no room even for regret, but only for the exhausted realization of a defeat, will be the cats of the poem *The cats will know,* written for the American starlet Constance 'Connie' Dowling at the end of their brief and unhappy love-affair. As it is well known, the woman he had nicknamed 'allodola americana' ('American lark') in order to emphasize her intrinsic elusiveness, had left him heartbroken after returning to New York, her home city. The heartfelt words that Pavese addresses to the "you" of this poem, in which his lover's face recalls once more the realm of Nature in the luxuriance of a melancholic spring season, not to mention the anaphoric repetition of the first verse, seem to mark the inexorable sinking into that existential whirlpool from which he will no longer be able to escape.

In a letter addressed to Doris Dowling, Connie's sister, some months before he commits suicide, the author confesses his abyssal loneliness by writing: "It's little comfort, Doris, being a genius: 'twere better for me to be a cat in N. Y., a swallow in Maine, a little ant under the slabs of a certain house in California" (Pavese 1966, 516). Once more, then, the comparison between his existential condition, which neither friendships nor professional success can relieve, and the animals 'supposed unawareness turns the animal world into a catalyzer of metaphysical meanings.

Similarly, a scratch on the door of the hotel room in which the female protagonist of the novel *Tra donne sole (Among Women Only,* 1950) commits suicide will prefigure the suicidal act carried out by the writer and ideally make the curtains fall on one of the most significant existential and literary events of the Twentieth century: "A cat had given her away – he was in the room with her, and the next day he miaowed and scratched so at the door that someone came and opened it" (Pavese 1959, 200).

5. Provisional conclusions:
a step ahead towards Pavese's animal acquaintance

This essay aimed to shine the first spotlight on Pavese's acquaintance of the animal world, providing several textual references to his main oeuvres, which demonstrate how meaningful the animal symbolism is in his literary output. In the first part of the paper, we tried to underline the hidden links existing between the development of his self-consciousness, both as a man and as a writer, and the "animal category", mostly seen from a physiological, ethnological or even psychoanalytical, point of view.

As we have seen so far, in Pavese's texts, the animal image always acquires an archetypical value and immediately becomes a vehicle of poignant textual and metatextual meanings, especially when the sudden contiguity between animal and human realm (see, for instance, the case of the *Dialoghi con Leucò*, where this topic is mostly addressed) leads to forms of hybridization.

In the second half, we found and contextualized several examples taken from Pavese's novels and poems, in order to emphasize how deep the animal image, as a bearer of meaning, sunk into his existential parable from the very beginning of his literary career to his dramatic suicidal act.

Bibliography

Barbarino, L. P. (2019). "Dall'erba' nasce «Lavorare stanca». Fogli e «Foglie» di Whitman all'inizio di Pavese: le giovanili, le carte, la 'princeps'", *Sinestesie*, 17, pp. 59-70

Borsari, E. (2000). "Cesare Pavese. Critica ai «miti della critica»", *Strumenti Critici*, 15(3), pp. 427-462

Braidotti, R. (2011). *Nomadic Theory: The Portable Rosi Braidotti*. New York: Columbia University Press

Grosz, E. (1994). *Volatile Bodies: Toward a Corporeal Feminism*. Bloomington: Indiana University Press

Guiducci, A. (1974). *Invito alla lettura di Pavese*. Milano: Mursia

Heiney, D. (1971). *The Smile of Gods. A Thematic Study of Cesare Pavese's Works* by G. P. Biasin, review, *Comparative Literature*, 23 (4), pp. 366-369

Jung, C. G. (1965). *La libido: simboli e trasformazioni*. Torino: Boringhieri

Lajolo, D. (1983). *The Absurde Vice. Biography of Cesare Pavese*, translated by M. and M. Pietralunga. New York: Norton & C.

Leake, E. (2014). *Cesare Pavese, Posthumanism, and the Maternal Symbolic* in Amberson, D. and Past, E. (eds.) *Thinking Italian Animals. Human and Posthuman in Modern Italian Literature and Film*. London: Palgrave Macmillan, pp. 39-56

Pavese, C. (1952b). *The Moon and the Bonfires*, translated by L. Sinclair. London: Lemann

—— (1956). *The House on the Hill*, translated by W. J. Strachan. London: Owen

—— (1959). *Among Women Only*, translated by D. D. Paige. New York: The Noonday Press

—— (1965). *Dialogues with Leucò*, translated by W. Arrowsmith and D. S. Carne-Ross. London: Owen

—— (1966). *Lettere 1945-1950*, Torino: Einaudi

—— (1976). *Hard Work*, translated by W Arrowsmith. New York: Grossman

—— (1999). *Dialoghi con Leucò*. Torino: Einaudi

—— (2009). *This Business of Living: Diaries 1935-1950*. London: Routledge

—— (2016). *Working Wearies. A retranslation of Pavese's* Lavorare Stanca, translated by E. Marpa. Rome: CreateSpace Independent Publishing Platform

Salvadori. D. (2017). "Protagonisti inconsapevoli: animali nella letteratura per l'infanzia e per ragazzi", *LEA. Lingue e letterature d'Oriente e d'Occidente*, 6, pp. 461-482

Sichera, A. (2015). *Pavese. Libri sacri, misteri, riscritture*. Firenze: Olschki

Trovato, M. C. and Barbarino, L. P. (2014). «*Non si sfugge alla selva: appunti per un alfabeto dantesco in Cesare Pavese*», in Bertini Malgarini, P.; Merola, N.; and Verbaro, C. (eds). *La funzione Dante e i paradgmi della modernità*. Atti XXVI Convegno MOD (Roma, Lumsa, 10-13 giugno 2014). Roma: ETS, pp. 433-442

Vignola, P. (2013) *Divenire animale. La teoria degli affetti di Gilles Deleuze tra etica ed etologia*, in Andreozzi, M. and Castiglione, S. (eds.) *Emotività animali. Ricerche e discipline a confronto*. Alma Massaro: LED, 117-124.

Whitman, W. (2017). *Foglie d'erba*, translated by M. Corona. Milano: Mondadori

Further Reading

Besson F.; Bora Z. M.; Marroum M.; Slovic S.; Kev R. K. (2021). *Reading Cats and Dogs: Companion Animals in World Literature*. Lanham, Lexington Books

Braidotti, R. (2013). *The Posthuman*. Cambridge: Polity Press

Derrida, J. (2008). *The Animal That Therefore I Am*. Ed. Marie-Luise Mallet. New York: Fordham University Press

Iovino, S. (2015). *Ecologia letteraria. Una strategia di sopravvivenza*. Milano: Edizioni Ambiente

Pavese, C. (1952a). *La letteratura americana e altri saggi*. Torino: Einaudi, 1952

Philipsson, P. (2006). *Origini e forme del mito greco*. Torino: Bollati Boringhieri

Smith, L. (2012). *Cesare Pavese and America: Love, Life, and Literature*. Amherst (MA): University of Massachusetts Press

Untersteiner, M. (1946). *La fisiologia del mito*. Torino: Bollati Boringhieri.

Chapter 3

The "donne vestite per gli occhi[1]" in Cesare Pavese's Creative Production

Monica Lanzillotta

Università della Calabria

Abstract

This essay re-interprets Pavese's poetic and narrative production to trace the specific figure of the prostitute. The writer depicts this figure thoroughly in his entire production, since his first poems until his last novel, describing many aspects of her role: from the physical appearance of many prostitutes to the places where they exercise their job. In Pavese's poetics, the figure of the prostitute embodies three main situations, all of them crucial in Pavese's production: the urban modernity; the *alter ego* of the Self; and the rite of passage from adolescence to maturity.

Keywords: prostitute, city, rite of passage, adult life, modernity

* * *

Prostitution is a social construction subject to various definitions and representations over the centuries, as well as the topic of an extensive critical literature ranging from sociology to politics, from literature to cinema. The oldest profession in the world was legal both in ancient Greece and in ancient Rome. In Italy, going to modern times, on February 15th, 1860, Camillo Benso di Cavour – at that time prime minister of the Kingdom of Sardinia, the first seed of the future Kingdom of Italy – authorized the opening of brothels in Lombardy under the State control. They were regulated by the royal decree *Regolamento del servizio di sorveglianza sulla prostituzione*, the act which extended prostitution to the whole country. Later, the Crispi law, approved on March 29th, 1888, banned brothels nearby, places of worship and schools and

---

[1] Literally, women «dressed to be seen»: the periphrasis to name prostitutes in the poem *Sultry Lands,* from *Hard Labor* (*Lavorare stanca*, 1936). See Pavese 1976, 30.

imposed the closure of their shutters; for this reason, brothels were named as "closed houses". During the twentieth century, brothels were eventually shut down for good by the Merlin law (from the name of the Socialist senator Lina Merlin who promoted this law) on September 20th, 1958.

In the late nineteenth century, the figure of the prostitute became central in the debates of the positivist scientific culture, especially in the field of criminal anthropology. Cesare Lombroso, founder of this discipline, equated prostitution with hereditary degeneration, therefore legitimizing the social control over the prostitute. *La donna delinquente, la prostituta e la donna normale,*[2] the treatise published by Cesare Lombroso and Guglielmo Ferrero in 1893, had a great echo (see Greco 1987, Montaldo 2019, and Azara-Tedesco 2019). In the same period, because of the increasing migration to the Americas and Asia, the white slavery phenomenon with the coerced prostitution of European women emerged (see Corbin 1982 and Gibson 1983). By the end of the century, with the overcoming of the Victorian *Zeitgeist*, scholars, painters, and composers from all over Europe restored high symbolic significance to the figure of the prostitute. A good example of how the Italian imagery was influenced by the literary ideal of French brothels – depicted and celebrated by writers and especially painters (such as Edgar Degas, Vincent Van Gogh, Édouard Manet, Paul Cézanne, Henri de Toulouse-Lautrec, Edvard Munch, and Émile Bernard) – is Guido Gozzano, who in the very famous poem *Cocotte*, names the prostitute under the French epithet.

From a very young age, Pavese perceived the horizons of Fascist cultural identity as very narrow and he opened up to ancient and modern cultures, engaging in translation. He loved to overcome and cross borders, enlarging boundaries to go beyond cultural hierarchies and distances. Before his official debut as a translator in 1931 (with *Il nostro signor Wrenn. Storia di un gentiluomo romantico*, the translation of Sinclair Lewis's 1914 novel *Our Mr. Wrenn. The Romantic Adventures of a Gentle Man*) and as a writer in 1936 (with *Lavorare stanca*, his first collection of poetry), he experimented, from 1922 to 1931, with almost any literary genre, as documented by critical notes, translations, tales, poems and other materials which were published posthumously.

Pavese was an open-minded reader and, as he wrote in a letter to his friend Tullio Pinelli dated August 18th, 1927, a "bookish man", who equates with books

---

[2] The book was first partially translated in English in 1895 by W. Douglas Morrison with the title *The Female Offender* (without the entire section on the normal woman). In 2004, N. H. Rafter and M. Gibson provided its complete translation with the title *Criminal Woman, the Prostitute, and the Normal Woman*.

("sees nothing but books, can no longer live apart from books, reasons through books, feels and loves, even sleeps with books": Pavese 1969, 47). His rigorous apprenticeship was characterized by readings, critical reflections, and translations of Italian and European literature classics, which provide him with models for his own poems and tales. He immersed himself in the reading of Latin poetry (in 1923-1925, he translated Ennius, Plautus, Terence, Lucilius, Lucretius, and especially Catullus, Virgil, and Horace), of fourteenth-century Italian lyric tradition (from Dolce Stil Novo to Dante and Petrarch), and nineteenth-century Italian poetry (he loved particularly Leopardi, Carducci, D'Annunzio, and the Crepusculars). Then, he studied both European and American preromantic and romantic poetry, translating between 1922 and 1929 English authors (Shakespeare, Macpherson, Barbauld, Burns, Wordsworth, Byron, Shelley, Keats, Browning and Arnold), American poets (Longfellow, Poe, and Walsh), German scholars (Klopstock, Herder, Goethe, Schiller, Hölderlin, Kleist, Uhland, Eichendorff, Rückert, Grillparzer, Körner, Von Platen-Hallerümnde, Heine, Lenau, and Freiligrath), and French writers (Hugo and Baudelaire). Pavese's poetic vocation manifested very early in his childhood: between 1919 and 1920, he composed his first poem dedicated to the Russian Revolution, entitled *Trotsky e Lenin van morti* (*Trotsky and Lening are dead*), and since 1922-1923 he started to write various tales and poems, imitating especially Dante, Petrarch, and Romantic scholars, with no original results. He started elaborating his own style between 1926 and 1930, when the Stil Novo and the Romantic poets gave way to the Decadent ones. The turning point was the immersive reading of Walt Whitman's *Leaves of Grass*. In a 1927 tale entitled *Wings Agitation*, for example, Pavese wrote that Whitman is his model as an iconoclast and incommensurable genius ("merciless iconoclast of the culture", "genius, endowed with an almost unfathomable originality") and that he feels the echo of some Decadent masters: "Hopelessly, Baudelaire, da Verona, Gozzano, all the immense decadence" (Pavese 1969, 246; 248). The prostitute figure enters Paves's creative production since 1928 through a very dense autobiographical model. The young writer fell in love without reciprocity with schoolmates, dancers, and actresses, and he aspires to become a great writer, although with no significant success. The high sense of failure as a man and as an artist brings him on the track of Baudelaire's *Fleurs du Mal*[3] and he gets in

---

[3] As Benjamin writes, prostitution colors especially ("colora in modo particolare") Baudelaire's poetry (Benjamin 1962, 142). Pavese translated the *Idéal* from the *Fleurs du mal* in May 1928 (see Pavese 2021a, 1222). On the relationship Pavese-Baudelaire, see Pertile 1970.

scene as poet *maudit*, relating to the figures of the beggar and the prostitute.[4] For example, he wrote to Giorgio Curti on October 22nd, 1926: "In spirit, I feel like a beggar. I keep on telling everyone about my inner suffering, just as beggars parade their sores and filth" (Pavese 1969, 35). If in his early work the figure of the prostitute is an *alter ego*, later Pavese will represent her as one of the main characters of urban modernity and as the embodiment of a rite of passage to adult life.

The setting of the early poetic and narrative work of the Piedmontese writer was the city of Turin in the early twentieth century, which was a city in transition towards industrialization and urbanization. The Piedmontese capital depicted by Pavese is a threatening giant, whose streets are populated by big houses, invaded by mobs, noises, and lights. It is very similar to the infernal city celebrated by Baudelaire or eternalized by American cinema and literature, especially by Whitman. Pavese wrote in 1926 to his friend Tullio Pinelli this letter, admitting his fascination for the city and the urban environment: "I myself (I don't know if it's due to the influence of Walt Whitman) wouldn't exchange a city like Turin for a couple of dozen country estates. [...] the real, modern life, as I dream of it and fear it, is a great city, full of noise, factories, houses, great palaces and silly, pretty women" (Pavese 1969, 31). The stage is that of the suburbs, working-class neighborhoods and factories or peripheral streets populated by marginal people (the beggar, the drunk, the unemployed, and so on), some of whom are selling the only good they have, which is their own body. The young Pavese mirrored himself in all these characters. In the poem *The Bright Fevers II* (1928), he eternalizes a dark street of Turin by night, where lost souls (the narrator, a beggar, and an unquiet whore) wander (a "dark street" full of "tormented souls", wandering "without direction": Pavese 2021a, 590). The full identification of the narrator with the prostitute is at the center of the poem *The Aversion against the Brothel* (1929):

> You poor soul, tired and embellished,
> we are lingering along crowded streets
> tired of a life not yet experienced
> and everyone is screaming at us,
> we are like the poor whores
> who stroll around,
> and whose aspect is a horrible mask.
> They clench between their lips
> the hoarse cigarette

---

[4] Pavese will gradually attribute to the beggar the types of Sophocles' *Oedipus* (see Lanzillotta 2011).

as a last, desperate handhold.
And in the nocturnal inn
they let themselves go drinking the dirty wine,
as red as their mouths.
In this way, I contemplate our ending,
solitary soul,
because the world will never answer to our tears
and, would we flare up, we are pitiful.
You glum, glum soul,
dying like a phthisic,
what could we ever drink tonight? (Pavese 2021a, 600)[5]

The lyric is from *Blues of the Big City*, the collection in which Pavese models his verses and prosody on the poems of Camillo Sbarbaro's poetic collection *Pianissimo*, published in 1914 by the Voce editions: the lyrics of *Blues of the Big City* are composed, like Sbarbaro's, mainly by hendecasyllables alternated to loose septenaries. *Pianissimo* is a prominent poetic work of Twentieth-century Italian literature in which the crisis of values brought about by WWI is anticipated not only in Italy but also in Europe, a pioneer work which describes man's disorientation and death of the soul.

In it, the descent into hell that characterizes the modern poetry is complete, almost at its most extreme results. During this descent, the man discovers himself more and more similar to a thing, an object. Starting from Beaudelaire's lesson, [Sbarbaro] describes, before Montale, the absence of life, the condition that makes a man a sleepwalker, witnessing astonished the apparitions of the world after having verified the death of the soul and having invoked his transfiguration into a mineral. (Polato 2001a, 12)

The main character of *Pianissimo* is a lonely sleepwalker who, like in the *Fleurs du Mal*, is *déraciné* without self-consciousness, stranger to things and mankind, wandering by night between brothels and taverns as places of perdition attended by prostitutes and drunks, with whom Sbarbaro identifies. In *The Aversion against the Brothel* the young Pavese seems to "imitate[6]" some rhymes of *Pianissimo*: *Be silent, my soul, weary as you are*, the first poetry in *Pianissimo* where Sbarbaro introduces the topics and the tone of the whole collection (Pavese draws from it the verses "The siren of the world / has lost its

---

[5] When not specified, all these translations into English were made by Iuri Moscardi.

[6] On the relationship between Sbarbaro and Pavese, see Lanzillotta 2017.

voice": Sbarbaro 1985, 78), and the poems where Sbarbaro identifies with prostitutes and drunks (*In my Poor Blood Sometimes*; *I Await You at the Turn of Every Street*; *When I Cross the City by Night*; *You So Slim, with Shiny Eyes*; and *Sometimes, While I Walk Along the Street*).[7] Prostitutes, hunting for tricks in Turin suburbs like lost dummies ("staggering, wandering, lost": Pavese 1976, 78), return also in the poems *Lost Women* (1931), *Workers of the World* (1932), and *Deola's Return* (1936).

In his poetic and narrative production, Pavese carefully portrays the prostitute's character, beginning with the places where she works: the prostitutes in Turin satisfy their clients on the road, in their miserable houses, or in institutionalized brothels. In *The Comrade* (1946), prostitutes hunt for tricks by night down corso Inghilterra saying "Give me a cigarette" (Pavese 1959, 83).[8] In *Among Women Only* (1949), prostitutes lure in via Calandra, in Porta Palazzo's dives, and in a run-down cafe with a dance floor and a small garden. The houses of the prostitutes are depicted in these poems and tales: in *Habitudes* (1936), where a man remembers when he met a prostitute in a quiet room; in *Two Cigarettes* (1933), where a prostitute has sex with clients lured on the road in the squalid flat where she lives; and in the tale *The Houses* (1942), where some prostitutes meet clients in the room of a run-down building in the center of Turin.

Houses of pleasures, mainly attended by young men never engaged, are represented in various poems and tales. They remind French houses, also because they are managed by women named as Madame: in the short story *Arcadia* (1929), Paolo, who is not engaged, attends houses of pleasure, a habit that he feels as depressing ("he does not consider it neither shameful nor sad. But it was depressing, terribly depressing"), while in the tale *Night Life or The Dialogue of the Lost Friendship* (1930) a brothel in Turin is vividly described and it looks very similar to those painted by Henri de Toulouse-Lautrec. This house is managed by Madame Adele, a curvy and sternly lady holding a big wallet, who welcomes clients in a red wallpapered living room decorated with dark, inlayed furniture. Four girls and two ladies come in:

---

[7] From the latter poem, Pavese seems to pick up prostitutes "painted" faces (Sbarbaro 1985, 52).

[8] Pablo, the protagonist of the novel *The Comrade*, meets a prostitute in the grove and says that she did everything ("She certainly did [to look after me]; she even did up my overcoat": Pavese 1959, 105). Luciano, one of Pablo's friends from Rome, tells that while working in Turin he had met a beautiful prostitute girl ("a marvellous tart": Pavese 1959, 148).

Light dresses, some provocative details, revealed by a gesture, a neckline; but, after all, old, fade limbs. No lust. Tired and painted faces. Among the other, one was young, childlike, but empty: a mask.
The girls were talking among themselves, as if they were alone [...] then, gathered close to the radiator, they continued their conversation. One girl turned on herself. Another one lifted her hose.

In the lyrics *Unconvinced People* (1933), the hard life of prostitutes working in brothels as in barracks ("like in the barracks") is emphasized. In the tale *The Idol* (1937), the brothel salon is described with clients sitting nearby the wall and two crossed-legs girls on the sofa ("two girls sitting on the divan with their bare legs wide apart": Pavese 1987, 260) while a fat half-naked girl, standing down the hall, talks to a sergeant. Houses of pleasures are present also in the tales *Suicides* (1937) and *Loyalty* (1938). In the latter, Pavese focuses on prices: Amelio, the main character, is paralyzed in bed after a motorcycle accident; when Natalina, the woman he dated before the accident, left him, he asked his friend Garofalo to bring a woman to his home. The friend goes to a brothel, but the *maîtresse* asks him too much money (one hundred liras), so he looks for a more affordable prostitute working on the street. Soon, in a peripheral road, he finds a dull face with eyes and mouth wide open ("a pale face that seemed all eyes and mouth": Pavese 1987, 328), who agrees to go to Amelio's the next day. Finally, in *The Harvesters* (1939), Talino does not go with one of the prostitutes of Madama Angela's brothel because prices are too high, and he turns to a cheaper girl in Bra.

In Pavese's works, not only prostitutes satisfy sexual needs and desire, but they also emerge as crucial to the rite of passage from adolescence to maturity. In the poem *Sultry Lands* (1935), a young man tells his friends from the countryside that he has seen on the road those malicious women, eye-candies, walking and smoking on their own ("sly flirtatious women, dressed to be seen, walking alone [...] they even smoke alone": Pavese 1976, 30). In the short tale *The Beggars* (1941), the rowdy teenager Achille, curious about adult life, often goes to a cafe attended by prostitutes and knows everything about brothels even if he has never attended one: "Still, he knew what to do, how much to pay and what to say to the doorkeeper" (Pavese 1987, 333). In the short tale *The City* (1942), the anonymous narrator is a university student who, before meeting her girlfriend Maria, had only been with prostitutes. In the short tale *The Houses* (1942), the young character has no experience with women and his friend Ciccotto brings him to a private house where prostitutes work. Finally, in *The Devil in the Hills* (1948), the narrator states that when young, he was always looking for girls in equivocal places ("I was always on the point of picking up a girl or sticking my nose into some alluring dive": Pavese 1968, 289).

Pavesian prostitutes are characterized by a few traits, which shamelessly reveal their identities: their voice is raspy because they drink and smoke, they have consumed lineaments and pale faces lit by red lipstick, they sit with their legs crossed while showing off in the brothel window or in the streets, and they wear bright-colored dresses. In the house of pleasures of *Night Life or The Dialogue of the Lost Friendship* (1930), a dark-hair girl with very red, expert lips shows up; in the poem *Dina Thinking* (1933), the character dresses in red to attract clients; in the short tale *The Idol* (1937), the prostitute Mina is very nice and neat in her dressing at the Turin brothel where she works, and while shopping she looks colorful and elegant ("She was wearing a pale blue brassiere and white silk panties", "her chestnut coat with buttons at the side", "wearing a striking, flame-colored cloak that made her stand out from the crowd", "in blue and orange": Pavese 1987, 270; 267; 283; 284).

Pavesian prostitute is mainly represented as an impassible woman, with no memory of sexual intercourses consumed. In *A Memory* (1935), for example, the writer portrays a promiscuous woman walking on the street with an "ambiguous" smile: she smiles faintly after the intercourse, too, and she always gives herself every time with untirable passion, as it were the first time ("No tiredness touches her": Pavese 1976, 69). Besides this type, there is the woman who prostitutes herself not only for money but also to satisfy her nymphomania. In the novel *The Beautiful Summer* (1940), Amelia works as a prostitute and seems to be affected by nymphomania as her sexual desire is insatiable. Being bisexual, she has intercourses with both men and women: she hunts for tricks in cafes, her legs crossed and her hand below her chin; on the road, she lures a disturbing man ("[his face] bore an ugly scar on the temple": Pavese 1955b, 206) as she knows he pays generously; and she hangs out with a painter, who wants to portray two women hugging each other ("This fool of an artist wanted to do a painting of two women embracing": Pavese 1955b, 185); she reveals to Ginia the fantasy of a lesbian threesome; she contracts syphilis from the painter and she has intercourses with Guido, Rodrigues, and Ginia's brother. Another nymphomaniac appears in *The Comrade* (1946), when Pablo tells that while driving the truck with his colleague, Milo, he had taken on board a girl down the street, and she had an intercourse with Milo while he was driving. According to Pablo, she was not a prostitute but rather a nymphomaniac, as he describes her in this way: "But she was not one of the dressed-to-kill types. She was not even painted. She seemed a homely woman between thirty and forty years old, with a lean face and hungry eyes" (Pavese 1959, 84).

Pavese also depicts prostitutes' enjoyment and dreams. In Turin, they often enjoy the morning time to relax and enjoy life in isolation. In the poem *Deola Thinking* (1932), 30-year-old Deola, whose clients are soldiers and workers

("workers and soldiers [...] who break your back"), enjoys mornings at the cafe ("spends her mornings sitting in the café": Pavese 1976, 33); in *Dina Thinking* (1933), she loves swimming naked in the river in the morning; the prostitute of the poem *Tolerance* (1935) drinks from the fountain at daybreak, staining water with her lipstick ("and the water is reddish": Pavese 1976, 31); the protagonist of *The Country Whore* (1937), awakening in the shabby and solitary brothel where she works, loves enjoying the scent of flowers and the warm rays of the sun entering from the open window, whose smell and warmth remind her of her childhood; finally, in the short tale *The Idol* (1937), the prostitute Mina, who works in a brothel, goes shopping in the morning and enjoys city shop-windows. Some prostitutes dream about quitting the profession and marrying a client. In the short tale *Along the Streets, at Night* (1926), Ninì, forced to prostitute as she is extremely poor, deceives herself when a young student dates her for a month, but her dreams crack when she sees the young man with a fine and elegant lady: she burst in tears, full of anger and envy. In the poem *Deola Thinking* (1932), the protagonist dreams to flee with the gentle and nice man ("businessman") she spent the night with (Pavese 1976, 33). Such a dream comes true for Mina, the ambitious protagonist of the short tale *The Idol* (1937), who marries an old engineer, a client of hers in the brothel where she works.

Besides him, other men who desire to marry prostitutes appear in Pavese's works. In the short tale *For Some Reasons* (1936) the writer, in the footsteps of Kafka's *The Trial*, represents the absurd vicissitudes of a scholar, denounced, and arrested because he does not work and is devoted to writing. Accused of economic inactivity ("Inattività economica"), after one month in prison, he can escape from condemnation either by working for two years in a state factory or by getting married in two months, as a wife guarantees for his husband's efficiency ("A wife is always a guarantee of efficiency of her husband"). Outside of the prison, he starts looking for a wife in ballrooms and equivocal cafes. One night he meets Ginetta, a slim, feline prostitute, and proposes her to marry him, affirming that she could continue her profession. Unfortunately, the woman tells him that she is already married to a less honest man than him, and the man will eventually get married thanks to the clerk who interrogated him: "You see [...]. I already found someone like you. It happened when I started this kind of life. He stalked me and he threw this job in my face. He wanted to redeem me. You are like him, but you are more honest. He adored me: I trusted him, and I married him. Now, I am still doing the same job and I must support him and me". In the short tale *The Idol* (1937), too, Guido would like to marry Mina, the girl he engaged with some years before, who works in a brothel in Turin.

In Pavese's works, prostitutes are criticized or feared, especially by other women, the only exception being the novel *The Beach* (1940-1941), where the young Berti defends the category because prostitutes advantage honest women in many respects: "That woman [the prostitute] was worth more than many well-brought-up girls, as, for that matter, was true of all her sort, who at least had one advantage in their hard lives over the proper ones", because men, going to prostitutes, "letting off steam [...] are protecting the others" (Pavese 1968, 34). Feminine hostility emerges, in particular, in the poem *Tolerance* (1935), where a prostitute arrived by train in a Southern village is feared by the local spouses, grim and worried about their husbands who could go to her. In *Among Women Only* (1949), too, prostitutes are at the center of conversations among Clelia and her friends Rosetta and Momina. During a road trip, Rosetta says she does not despise prostitutes but prefers women who work and, when Clelia replies that also prostitutes work, Momina says that prostitutes have a stupid face. The three friends go back to the topic some days later, when Momina calls her friend Nene a whore because she wants to appear different than she is:

> [...] intelligent, she has her craft at her fingertips, and all the temperament a sculptress could have. Why doesn't she stick to that? But no. She has to dress like a child, fall in love, get drunk. One of these days there'll be a baby. She has the face for it ... She thinks that others fall for her babyishness. (Pavese 1968, 260)

Clelia agrees with Momina ("It's the work you do that counts, not how you do it") and Momina sums up everything by saying that all women are considered as whores: "I don't know what counts [...]. I'm afraid nothing counts. We're all whores" (Pavese 1968, 260). The three friends play whores a few days later: after drinking at a party in the studio of the painter Loris, they go with other friends to an equivocal tavern in Calandra street to watch the brothel clients nearby, then everything degenerates through jokes and equivocal bets.

> Laughing and shouting, they said we should be tested and compared and have our points entered on a score card. So they started arguing which one of us would make the best prostitute; for gifts both of body and soul, the hunchback added. Mariella, too, was discussed and she ended by getting angry and taking the score card seriously. She nearly fought with Momina. But the old painter said we were all meritorious, that it was a matter of time and tastes; the real criterion should be our price and the sort of place we worked in.
> Someone tried to suggest theater and nightclub stages. "No, no," the hunchback said, "We're talking about real whorehouse houris." (Pavese 1968, 271)

Pavese eternalizes not only prostitutes in the city of Turin, but also those working in Piedmont villages and in Southern Italy. In Piedmont, beside the brothel in Bra recalled in *The Harvesters*, the Langhe town of Canelli is so relevant for the presence of prostitutes that it is considered almost as equivalent as Paris. In *Ciau Masino* (1930-1932), Masino, a car tester at Fiat in Turin fired after taking over a drunk peasant, gets a job in the Langhe, at don Rôss' motor pool; there, to satisfy his sexual hunger he goes to Canelli-Paris ("He decided to go to Canelli – Paris – and to spend what was necessary [...]. He asked Don Rôss for a day off and fifty liras" and then he came back in the evening "with fifteen liras remaining"). Canelli is also recalled in the novel *The Moon and the Bonfires* (1950), when the young Anguilla finds out that the owner of a brothel in Canelli used a gambit to attract customers, bringing three or four women to stroll downtown on coach:

> There was an open carriage showed up in Canelli every now and then with three or even four women in it, and these women would take a leisurely drive through the streets, as far as the Station, and Sant'Anna, up and down the main road, stopping for drinks in the cafés here and there – all so as to be seen by the men, to attract customers, it was their boss's idea, and then anyone who was old enough and had the money could go to a certain house in Villanova and sleep with one of them. (Pavese 2021b, 77)

As for Southern villages, in the poem *Tolerance* (1935) a prostitute, arrived by train in an anonymous Southern village on the seafront, goes to live in a "blackened house" (Pavese 1976, 31). In the tale *Land of Exile* (1936) and the novel *The Political Prisoner* (1938-1939), where Pavese sets events and experiences of his political confinement in Brancaleone, the same pattern returns: in another Southern village, some men get a prostitute from the city, paying her to be available to everybody for a few days. In the tale, the prostitute's name is Concetta, depicted by the contrast between her dark skin and her blond hair ("her dark, greasy skin and the exotic fineness of her fair hair": Pavese 1987, 25); in the novel, the prostitute's name is Annetta, who is small and plump, vicious and innocent ("that plump figure with hair tumbling untidily about her shoulders and her pink brassière with its consumptive embroidery": Pavese 1955a, 120). Concetta lives in the butcher's shop and is well fed, "on meat and olives" (Pavese 1987, 24), while Annetta stays in a shabby small room in the tailor's house:

> The tiny room had a sloping ceiling and the woman was sitting on the rumpled bed in her camisole, showing her bare shoulders. She was eating from a soup plate with a spoon. She raised her placid eyes to meet

them, balancing the plate on her lap. Her feet did not reach the ground,
ant it made her look like a rather plump child. [...]
Gaetano went up to her and pinched her cheek between his fingers. The
woman withdrew her head pettishly, and having deposited the spoon
on the floor, placed her hands on her knees, and stared expectantly at
the three men with what she imagined was a smile. (Pavese 1955a, 117-
118)

The central topic of Pavese's works is the passage from adolescence to
adulthood, which the author develops through two geographic poles: the
countryside (the Langhe) and the city (Turin). In *Notes on Certain Unwritten
Poems*, composed in February 1940 and published in 1943 in the second edition
of *Lavorare stanca* (*Hard Labor*), he describes the parable of many of his
characters as the adolescent adventure from the countryside to the city, where
sex is a false remedy to loneliness: "The adventure of the adolescent boy who is
proud of the countryside where he lives and who imagines that the city will be
like the country. But in the city, he discovers loneliness and tries to cure it with
sex and passion; but they only uproot him and alienate him from city and
country alike, leaving him in a more tragic loneliness which marks the end of
adolescence" (Pavese 1976, 110). Pavese's adolescents establish a contact with
the Mother Earth, often walking barefoot and craving for sun naked in the grass,
woods, and on the hilltops. Blending in grass, mud, dew, they regress to the
animal and vegetal reign. Earth and land in Pavese are linked, since the
beginning of his creative production, to the female body, with a Dannuntian
sensitivity: the verb *imbestiarsi* (to mingle with beasts), borrowed from Dante,
is used by D'Annunzio and Pavese as "a key to his own poetic" ("a cardine della
propria poetica": Costa 1989, 152). Pavese's woman-earth is a jealous and
demanding lover, she does not tolerate betrayals, as sexuality does not belong
to the childish domain. The prostitute, fully depicted by Pavese from her
appearance to the places where she works, is indeed deeply rooted in adult and
urban horizons, and represents a medium to reach adulthood and life maturity.

Since the very beginning of his literary career, Pavese was deeply attracted to
the figure of the prostitute, which in the Nineteenth century had already
acquired literary and artistic traits thanks to poets and painters. Pavese
depicted prostitutes in a very accurate way, from an external point of view, and
by identifying with them. In his poems, tales, and novels, he portrayed their
physical aspect, their dresses, their behavior, their enjoyments and dreams,
and their place of work. This fascination was due – during his juvenile years –
to Pavese's discovery and representation of life in the modern city of Turin. To
better represent the urban modernity, Pavese mirrored himself in the
prostitute, who become an *alter ego* of the Self. Later in his production, the
figure of the prostitute will shift from the sex worker who satisfies needs and

desires to embody a rite of passage to adult life. Pavese represented this passage through the two poles of the countryside and the city: the first, embodied by the Langhe, is the place where the young can feel the presence of a mysterious woman-earth, a demanding lover that can be reached only through the contact with the savage (beasts, sun, mud, water). On the contrary, the prostitute is rooted in adult and urban horizons, embodied by Turin, and represents a medium to reach adulthood and life maturity.

Bibliography

Benjamin, W. (1962). *Angelus Novus*. Torino: Einaudi

Costa, S. (1989). *Pavese e D'Annunzio*, in Ioli, G. (ed.) *Cesare Pavese oggi*. Regione Piemonte-Assessorato alla Cultura: San Salvatore Monferrato, 147-158

Pavese, C. (1955a). *The Political Prisoner*, translated by W. J. Strachan. London: Owen

——— (1955b). *The Beautiful Summer*, translated by W. J. Strachan. London: Owen

——— (1959). *The Comrade*, translated by W. J. Strachan. London: Owen

——— (1961). *This Business of Living, Diary: 1935-1950*, translated by A. E. Murch. London: Owen

——— (1968). *The Selected Works of Cesare Pavese*, translated by R. W. Flint. New York: Farrar, Straus and Giroux

——— (1969). *Selected Letters 1924-1950*, edited and translated by A. E. Murch. London: Owen

——— (1976). *Hard Labor*, translated by W. Harrowsmith. New York: Viking Press

——— (1987). *Stories*, translated by A. E. Murch. New York: The Ecco Press

——— (2021a). *L'opera poetica. Testi editi, inediti, traduzioni*, a cura di A. Sichera e A. Di Silvestro. Milano: Mondadori

——— (2021b). *The Moon and the Bonfires*, translated by T. Parks. London: Penguin Classics

Polato, L. (2001a). *Introduzione*, in Sbarbaro, C. *Pianissimo*, a cura di L. Polato. Venezia: Marsilio, pp. 11-36

Sbarbaro, C. (1985) *The Poetry and Selected Prose of Camillo Sbarbaro*. Edited and translated by V. Felaco. Potomac: Scripta Humanistica

Further Reading

Azara, L.-Tedesco, L. (eds.) (2019). *La donna delinquente e la prostituta. L'eredità di Lombroso nella cultura e nella società italiane*. Roma: Viella

Corbin, C. (1982), *Les filles de noce. Misère sexuelles et prostitution: 19ème et 20ème siècle*, Paris: Flammarion

Gibson, M. (1983). *Prostitution and the State in Italy 1860- 1915*. New Brunswick: Rutgers University Press

Greco, G. (1987). *Lo scienziato e la prostituta*. Bari: Dedalo

Lanzillotta, M. (2011). *«Andare per le strade giorno e notte a modo nostro senza mèta»: il mendicante nell'opera di Pavese*, in Lanzillotta, M. (ed.) *Cesare Pavese tra cinema e letteratura.* Soveria Mannelli: Rubbettino, pp. 151-214

——— (2017). *Il rapporto Sbarbaro-Pavese*, in Cavallini, E. (ed.) *Scrittori che traducono scrittori. Traduzioni 'd'autore' da classici latini e greci nella letteratura italiana del Novecento.* Alessandria: Edizioni dell'Orso, pp. 175-180

Montaldo, S. (2019). *Donne delinquenti. Il genere e la nascita della criminologia.* Roma: Carocci

Pertile, L. (1970). "Pavese lettore di Baudelaire", *Revue de littérature comparée*, XLIV (3), pp. 333-355

Polato, L. (2001b). *Commento e note ai testi*, in Sbarbaro, C. *Pianissimo*, a cura di L. Polato. Venezia: Marsilio, pp. 83-158

Chapter 4

Cesare Pavese the Americanist translator: A Chronology of the Myth

Kim Grego
Università degli Studi di Milano

Abstract

Cesare Pavese (1908-1950) is celebrated as a major figure in contemporary English-into-Italian (literary) translation, and as the one who introduced Twentieth-century American authors into Italy. However, although he translated between 1931 and his death, in 1950, he only did so regularly between 1931 and 1942. This essay sets out to propose a more objective chronological positioning of Pavese's translating work within the cultural phenomenon known as *americanismo*. It does so by reviewing, firstly, Italian 'Americanism' as it was ignited, spread and promoted by successive generations of translators, who brought contemporary American literature into Italy. It then moves on to evaluate Pavese's role in this cultural episode and, finally, proposes a re-positioning of his undisputed relevance within it. According to this chronological analysis of his translating activity, then, what emerges is that Pavese's part in the Americanist phenomenon was as pivotal as it was limited in time and scope. Therefore, while he cannot possibly be ignored when studying *l'americanismo*, neither can he be considered the sole figure behind its beginning and, especially, its end, as has been suggested by some critics.

Keywords: Cesare Pavese, traduzione, Translation Studies, americanismo, myth, Einaudi

* * *

1. Cesare Pavese's translations: all of them

Cesare Pavese (1908-1950) is celebrated as a major figure in contemporary English-into-Italian (literary) translation, and as the one who introduced

Twentieth-century American authors into Italy.[1] However, his work as a translator took place over nineteen years, i.e., between 1931 and 1950 – when he tragically took his own life –, but he only translated regularly and continuously between 1931 and 1942. Indeed, all his American translations were completed in this eleven-year period. Not only, the complete set of Pavese's translations (Table 4.1) amounts to 20 books,[2] mostly fiction but also essays, of which only 11 were authored by Americans, while the rest were by British writers, with the occasional translation from ancient Greek of authors such as Homer and Hesiod.

Table 4.1

Year of transl.	Author	Italian title	Original title	Original language	Year of publication of original
1931	Lewis, Sinclair	*Il nostro signor Wrenn*	*Our Mr Wrenn*	English, American	1914
1932	Melville, Herman	*Moby Dick*	*Moby Dick*	English, American	1851
1932	Anderson, Sherwood	*Riso nero*	*Dark Laughter*	English, American	1925
1933	Joyce, James	*Dedalus*	*The Portrait of the Artist as a Young Man*	English, British	1914-15 (installments)
1934	Dos Passos, John	*Il 42° parallelo*	*The 42nd Parallel*	English, American	1930
1937	Dos Passos, John	*Un mucchio di quattrini*	*The Big Money*	English, American	1936
1938	Steinbeck, John	*Uomini e topi*	*Of Mice And Men*	English, American	1937

[1] This work is partially inspired to the original thesis: Kim Grego, "Cesare Pavese traduttore: fra mito e realtà" (University of Bologna, 2001).

[2] To these, Mesiano adds the translations of Walt Whitman's poems *The Wallabout Martyrs* (published 1945), *A Passage to India* (incomplete) (published 2005), and diary *Specimen Days* (excerpts; published 1948) (Mesiano 2007, 64-65). Two Walt Disney. *Micky Mouse* comic books are only attributed to Pavese as their possible translator (Mesiano 2007, 61). Since these translations (not their publication) are not dated or attributed precisely (*A Passage to India* is reported in Pietralunga 2005, 115 to have been preparatory work for Pavese's thesis, from the years 1925-1930), they have been considered not fully pertinent to the arguments about the translating activity of Pavese as presented in this work.

Year of transl.	Author	Italian title	Original title	Original language	Year of publication of original
1938	Defoe, Daniel	*Fortune e sfortune della famosa Moll Flanders*	*Moll Flanders*	English, British	1722
1938	Stein, Gertrude	*Autobiografia di Alice Toklas*	*Autobiography of Alice B. Toklas*	English, American	1933
1939	Dawson, Christopher	*La formazione della unità europea dal secolo V all'XI*	*The Making of Europe*	English, British	1932
1939	Dickens, Charles	*David Copperfield*	*David Copperfield*	English, British	1849-50 (a puntate)
1940	Melville, Herman	*Benito Cereno*	*Benito Cereno*	English, American	1856
1940	Stein, Gertrude	*Tre esistenze*	*Three Lives*	English, American	1909
1940	Trevelyan, George	*La rivoluzione inglese del 1688-89*	*The English Revolution 1688-89*	English, British	1938
1941	Morley, Christopher	*Il cavallo di Troia*	*The Trojan Horse*	English, American	1937
1942	Faulkner, William	*Il borgo*	*The Hamlet*	English, American	1940
1947	Henriques, Robert	*Capitano Smith*	*Captain Smith and Company*	English, British	1943
1950	Toynbee, Arnold	*La civiltà nella storia* (compendio di D. Somervell, trad. in collaborazione con C. De Bosis)	*A Study of History* (abridgment by D. Somervell)	English, British	1947

Year of transl.	Author	Italian title	Original title	Original language	Year of publication of original
1981[3]	Hesiod / Homer	*La teogonia di Esiodo e tre inni omerici*		Greek, classic	VIII-VII sec. a.C.
1997[4]	Shelley, Percy Bysshe	*Prometeo slegato*	*Prometheus Unbound*	English, British	1820

Cesare Pavese's translations. It includes the works that Pavese translated from Greek and those posthumously published. It also differentiates between those from American (in grey) and from British English.

Is the myth of Pavese 'the Americanist' translator, then, actually justified, and/or is it still viable? This paper reviews and investigates the unquestionable role and relevance of Pavese as a translator, without in any way diminishing its linguistic, literary, and cultural significance, but hopefully proposing a more objective chronological positioning of it within the cultural phenomenon known as *americanismo*.

2. The Italian 'golden age' of American translations

Pavese, together with Elio Vittorini, Eugenio Montale, Alberto Moravia, and Giaime Pintor, to name but a few, contributed to the great translating activity that took place in Italy starting from the 1930s and which revolved around above all one theme: America.[5] This, indeed, was the period associated with the so-called Italian 'Americanism'. A phenomenon now well identified and widely described, it refers to the penetration of American culture into Europe in general and Italy in particular, through the works of American novelists from the first decades of the Twentieth century. Dominique Fernandez, in his influential essay on the American myth as spread in Italy through translations (see Fernandez 1969), places it between 1930-1950.[6] In doing so, Fernandez

---

[3] Posthumously published.

[4] Posthumously published.

[5] For historical, cultural and literary reasons, the nouns "America," "Americanism," the adjectives "American," "Americanist," etc. will be used here as synonyms of "United States of America," "USA," and "US," although the latter will be preferred when referring to the country as a political entity.

[6] Although several other scholars have written about Pavese's translations, it is believed that Fernandez's work contributed to establish a chronology seldom contested ever since.

seems to hold Pavese responsible for starting the myth of overseas literature in his country, and to have the phenomenon's end coincide, emblematically, with Pavese's death. Fernandez's view, laid out at the end of the 1960s, has continued to exert its influence to this day, e.g., in the words of Marina Guglielmi who, in the 1990s, were still based on the great French scholar's definition of "ventennio americano" and even proposed a debatable Pavese's "poetics of translation" (Guglielmi 1995, 301; 310). In Maria Walford-Dellù's 2002 review of literary criticism of Pavese from the 1940s to the 2000s (Walford-Dellù 2015), there also emerges a similar, uninterrupted trend, well into the new century. Clearly, there were several other events that contributed to the rise and fall of the Americanist myth of those decades. Some reflections on such dates will be proposed later on. For the moment, suffice it to observe that, while it is perhaps inaccurate to have the Americanist phenomenon coincide exactly with Pavese's translating activity, for sure, those experiences were closely connected.

Who else, then, was involved in the making of the myth? Some names were mentioned before but, to name the main protagonists of the Americanist myth, both in the US and in Italy, it is enough to look at the contents page of a single book: *Americana* (Vittorini 1941). Its title alone is a manifesto: without any specifications whatsoever, for the first time, someone intended to introduce America and its literature to Italians in a comprehensive and 'neutral' way, dropping any adjectives and prejudices that may be attached to them. That person was Elio Vittorini, and we shall later see that, in fact, his intended objectivity (if ever such objectivity really existed in his intentions) quickly evaporated, as the young editor's enthusiasm for the 'new world literature' could hardly be contained:

> Even when imagining a history of American literature the first word that comes to mind, and stops in front of us, and stops us, is earth itself. [...] So it is America that we say. We say it, and we see on the atlas the immensity of populated colors, the plains, the mountains, the sublime snows on the mountains and, high up north, the sea ice, and miles and miles of coasts facing two oceans with two great names, the Atlantic, the Pacific, and in all this the ancient god, the desert, and the waterways, the iron railways, the asphalt roads, the houses, the houses, the houses. (Vittorini 1941, 2)

The table of contents of *Americana* features some of the main American writers, from Washington Irving, Nathaniel Hawthorne and Edgard A. Poe, to

---

For this reason, this work focuses on it as a milestone in the criticism of Pavese the translator, as fundamental as – it is suggested – open to chronological clarifications.

Mark Twain and Herman Melville, to the contemporaries of Vittorini and Pavese themselves, preferably represented by short stories and novellas, but also by excerpts from novels. No less rich is the list of translators: symbolically placed at the beginning of the book, next to that of the authors – thus the editor acknowledged the translating profession to which he also belonged – it includes Carlo Linati, Guido Piovene, Eugenio Montale, Alberto Moravia, Cesare Pavese, and Vittorini himself.[7] This list certainly does not report all the Americanist translators who were active at the time,[8] but it does feature some of the most significant among them. This, not only because they translated, but also because they were – or were to become – accomplished authors of their own. *Americana* was first published in 1941: Linati already was an established writer, Americanist and translator; Montale had published his second major collection of poems with Einaudi (see Montale 1939) and was well known among the Florentine intellectual circle revolving around the literary magazine *Solaria*; but Moravia, Vittorini and Pavese, who were almost the same age, were just beginning to be known to the public. Of the three, Moravia had been the first to achieve some literary success, with his 1929 novel *Gli indifferenti*, but Vittorini and Pavese respectively published, in that very 1941, their most important work (*Conversazione in Sicilia*)[9] and very first novel (*Paesi tuoi*).[10] They were therefore young writers, at the beginning of their careers yet not completely unknown to the public, and already branded as opposers of the fascist regime.[11] Above all, they were enthusiastic about their American colleagues. These favorable circumstances all contributed to the creation of the myth of American literature in Italy, which arose precisely in connection with and around the time of the publication the first edition of Vittorini's *Americana*

---

[7] Billiani also mentions, in her review of foreign literature and culture imported into Italy between 1903 and 1943, "Praz, Soldati, e moltissimi traduttori rimasti praticamente sconosciuti," as well as "una schiera di valenti traduttori, che erano a loro volta scrittori, intellettuali o docenti universitari: Alvaro, Banfi, Bo, Camerino, Cecchi, Izzo, Lo Gatto, Montale, Moravia, Pavese, Pintor, Praz, Savinio e Zavattini" (Billiani 2007, 209-210).

[8] Ferme mentions, in passing, the other non-literati "sconosciuti traduttori prezzolati" who contributed to importing high and low American fiction into Italy in those years, among whom "due sconosciuti come Gastone Rossi e Attilio [*sic*; Alfredo?] Pitta" (Ferme 2002, 221; 55), who had manual jobs and translated part-time, for money.

[9] Vittorini's *Il garofano rosso* had already been published in *Solaria* in instalments in 1936, but *Conversazione in Sicilia*, first released in *Letteratura* in 1938-1939 and then republished twice as a volume in 1941, was the novel that made him successful.

[10] *Paesi tuoi* (1941) was the first novel published by Pavese. Previously, he had published the poetry collection *Lavorare stanca*, in 1936.

[11] Pavese was deported to the South of Italy in 1935-1936. Around the same time, Vittorini had been expelled from the Fascist Party for his views on the Spanish Civil War.

– the one that was seized by censors for its editor's excessively enthusiastic preface. Finally, another actor in the creation of "the so-called 'myth of America', passionately promoted by the work of people like Pavese e Vittorini" was "[l]'esigenza di affermarsi di nuovi editori come Bompiani, alla ricerca di voci nuove e di una contemporaneità che ad altri sembrava sconsigliabile sia per l'incertezza della reazione del pubblico, sia per i problemi di censura che poneva necessariamente un uso – anche linguistico – più spregiudicato del nostro" (Esposito 2018, 61).

Since 1941, the Americanism of those years has been widely studied from the multiple angles from which this cultural phenomenon may be seen. Some have emphasized the American literary influence on the language, genre, and structure of the European novel.[12] Others have linked it with the myth of those Italians who emigrated to the United States.[13] Others still have chosen a political approach to the problem, investigating the reasons why Marxist intellectuals nurtured a contradictory passion for capitalist and individualist America. Lastly, there have been those who have underlined the editorial importance of the phenomenon: the control exercised by the fascist censorship greatly influenced the choices of publishers, who were subject to the regime's rules restricting the publication of foreign works, many of which, such as American novels, were considered potentially subversive.[14] Those who have examined Cesare Pavese's activity as an Americanist have done so from one or more of these perspectives. Here, a more philological approach, based on his translations, shall be adopted, in order to describe the conditions that favoured the rise of Americanism, and to establish its chronological limits and define the role that Pavese played in it.

3. Once upon a time in America – Italian style

It would be interesting to compare what was happening in both Italy and America in 1930-1950, but it would be of little use to this work's purpose, since the Americanism of that period was an all-Italian phenomenon. It is not as

---

[12] See Carducci 1973 and Cartasegna 1952, 429-434.

[13] "The beginning of the new century saw new narrative experiments on the theme of emigration to America. They are mostly aimed at ideally combining, between Italy and its overseas double, American experiences with the (Italian) national literary scene, already compromised, as seen, by not a few poetic exercises, both cultured and popular, increasingly manneristic and ready to lead to the deplorable cliché of nostalgic self-pity" (Franzina 1996, 127; author's translation).

[14] Nonetheless, the translation rate remained high (about 10 percent of all the titles printed every year) until 1938, despite the fascist press campaigns, as mentioned by Ragone 1999, 161, note 13.

though US novels, in those years, were only translated into Italian, of course; they were successfully turned into French, for instance, as Sapiro 2016 illustrates through Faulkner's case. What made *Italian* Americanism unique was, perhaps obviously but worth stressing, the socio-historical setting in which it was planted and developed. By means of example, like France, Italy had seen people emigrate to the United States and it got involved in World War II; unlike France, Italy had its own specific relationship with American emigration, due to the high numbers involved (while "France contributed only a modest number": Haines 2000, 77) and specificities such as its infamous mafia connections; additionally, it was on the losing side during the war: all this resulted in the unique value and understanding of the American myth among the Italian readers of the period. Dunnett discusses the limits and boundaries of the definition of *americanismo* (she even provides an enjoyable lexicographic review of the related terms, from *americanismo* to *americanata* (Dunnett 2015, 42), and how it hardly manages to well represent such a complex, articulated experience. Like all myths, it was fuelled by the anxieties and desires of people completely extraneous to it, people who only indirectly knew what they held in such a high regard and who, consequently, ended up offering a distorted version of the original. It would rather be more appropriate to focus on the *idea* that the Italian intellectuals had of America at the time, since that idea was what Pavese and Vittorini had in mind when they 'discovered' their own America, and because the one they created, no matter the opinion of those who either exalted or censored their work, was an altogether *different* idea.

To begin with, Italians had, in those years, a generally cursory view of the United States. Three sources of information may be identified as those that mainly influenced the public's view of America at the time. The first is a popular source: the stories told by and about Italian emigrants. As is sadly known, even and especially in popular culture, migrations from Italy to the Americas were massive during the Giolitti governments,[15] reaching a peak in 1913, and continued throughout the first half of the Twentieth century. They mainly involved Southern Italians (but not only), forced to leave *en masse* by their stagnant rural economy and by the government's indifference to it. Those who had emigrated at the end of the Nineteenth or at the beginning of the Twentieth century had already started to improve their conditions, and began to return to Italy in 1920-1930. If they decided to remain in their new countries, they would send back money and tales of fabulous and rapid fortunes, of unlimited resources, of great opportunities for success (see Dunnett 2015, 43 on the

---

[15] Giovanni Giolitti served as President of Italy's Council of Ministers, on and off, between 1892 and 1921.

proverbial 'zio d'America'). Thus, although the legendary fortunes were relatively modest, a myth in its own right was created which, because it spread among uneducated and desperately poor peasants, grew out of all proportion, fed by accounts from both sides of the Atlantic. The second source was represented by the Italians' historical knowledge of America, nourished as much by the press of the time, as by the legacies of ancient travel literature. These were replenished with all the Eurocentric prejudices which, since Christopher Columbus's times, did not begin to fade until the end of the World War II, when the economic supremacy of the United States imposed its culture on the rest of the world. Hence, the news that appeared in the newspapers, about Henry Ford as well as jazz, on the crack of 1929 as on Sacco and Vanzetti, got blended, in the imaginary of the more educated readers, with their memories of Chateaubriand's *Atala*, Hawthorne's *Scarlet Letter*, to the most recent *American Classics* by D.H. Lawrence. And yet Italy, only recently turned into one independent country despite its North-South economic and cultural divide, and still not speaking a single national language, seemed in those years more committed to solving its enormous internal problems than to looking abroad with curiosity or for inspiration. Only major international events that had inevitable repercussions on the country did reach the entire population: among those, the two World Wars that marked the Twentieth century. The first close encounters with Americans indeed only occurred during World War I, followed by the Spanish Civil War, which saw the involvement of numerous Italians on either side. For the general public, however, America remained very distant, much more approachable through books than for real, and thus lending itself to the development of myths and mirages. Lastly, among those who contributed to making America known, were those whom Fernandez refers to as the "first generation of Americanists", or the "older Americanists in the [translating] trade" (Fernandez 1969, 112; 16): Carlo Linati, Mario Praz and Emilio Cecchi. These are systematically compared by Fernandez to Pavese and Vittorini (whom he labels the second generation of Americanist translators) as the opponents of the myth, only interested in American writers for the sole purpose of demoting and looking down on them from their own august Italianness. Actually, it is widely acknowledged that the first to import the contemporary American narrative into Italy were precisely the three writers from the 'old generation'. Not only, since they were no obscure authors that only translated for money or to have their names published, they were bound to have nurtured at least some genuine interest in the Americans whose works they translated.[16] To name but some names, Cecchi translated, among others,

---

[16] Some might say that translating for money is part of being a professional translator. On the contrary, translating for money was what most professional translators did. What I

William Faulkner, William Saroyan, T.S. Eliot; Linati: Henry James, O. Henry and Ezra Pound; Praz: T.S. Eliot and Henry Miller. However, an interest toward American authors, although very limited, had existed for a long time. Agostino Lombardo identifies Enrico Nencioni's *Saggi critici di letteratura inglese*, published in the second half of the Nineteenth century, as the first Italian critique of American literature:

> [...] the critic's interest in American literature started precisely with Nencioni (just as he was the one to start or at least consolidate the critical interest in English literature). Between 1867 and 1896 this greatly refined and cultivated scholar, of whom Carducci was a friend and an admirer, indeed wrote somewhat regularly, for *Nuova Antologia*, essays and reports about English and American literature. (Lombardo 1961, 13-14; author's translation)

Lombardo also reports that Giosuè Carducci, Giovanni Pascoli (influenced, he states, by Henry Wadsworth Longfellow and E.A. Poe) and Gabriele D'Annunzio (who for sure admired Walt Whitman) were the very first Italian intellectuals to express an interest in the literature coming from across the Atlantic – thus, long before Pavese and Vittorini, but also years ahead of Cecchi, Linati, and Praz. Not only, apart from the latter three, there were other *letterati* who were curious about things American, whether concerning the country itself or its literature. Two such people were Giuseppe Prezzolini and Giovanni Papini.

Prezzolini spread, in his many essays about America, a very critical view of the country, although not necessarily a negative one. In fact, he sometimes forced himself to provide the Italian public with an objective view of it. In a paper titled "Tre pregiudizi italiani", he tried to deconstruct some stereotypes usually associated with US people:

> The second prejudice [out of the three reported in the title] is that Americans are so ignorant that everything is good for them: the fake painting, the silly speech, the singer without a voice, the professor without a doctrine, watered-down wine and nobles who do not even feature in the Heraldic List. (Prezzolini 1958b, 31; author's translation)

---

wanted to express here is that the three authors mentioned (Linati, Praz, and Cecchi) were well established intellectuals who could afford *not* to translate for money. For this reason, their choices of books to translate ought to have been genuine.

Elsewhere in Prezzolini's work, nonetheless, there are echoes of the Europeans' traditional prejudices against America, although he was no occasional visitor to the US, having lived there for over forty years, from 1925 to 1968, while also lecturing at Columbia University, New York:

> The average American is ignorant of many things, and that is, in general, of everything that does not directly concern the profession he exercises: the average American is more ignorant, always speaking in general, than the average European, although in his own profession he is very often more competent, accurate and specialized. (Prezzolini 1958a, 45)

Of particular interest is a note by Prezzolini about the constant rivalry between the old and the new world, the latter calling the former *barbari*, a key-term, together with *feroce* and *furioso*, of Italian Americanism: "Having escaped from Europe, to avoid the pressure of history, the average American would not want more history to be made in other countries, and is inclined to consider his own ignorance and disinterest in foreign policy as a sign of political superiority and of moral elevation. Those poor barbarians from Europe!" (Prezzolini 1958a, 46; author's translation). All these adjectives were greatly exploited by its supporters to depict, on the contrary, the *positive* aspects that they saw in the American spirit, as opposed to Europe. In this light should Vittorini's famous words "He understood what the *strength* for man was in America, he understood the *ferocity*" (Vittorini 1941, 4; emphasis added) be read. Pavese himself, though less prone to his Sicilian colleague's 'fury', wrote in that period:

> Towards 1930, when fascism was beginning to be "the hope of the world", so it happened that some young Italians discovered America in his books, a pensive and *barbaric* America, happy and *quarrelsome*, *dissolute, fruitful, burdened* with all the past of the world, and at the same time young, innocent. [...] The taste of scandal and easy heresy that enveloped the new books and their themes, the *revolutionary fury* and sincerity that even the most foolish felt *throbbing* in those translated pages proved irresistible to an audience not yet completely dumbed by conformity and the academia. (Pavese 1951b, 193; emphasis added, author's translation)

Giovanni Papini, too, was attracted to the 'barbarianism' of American literature. In particular, he admired Walt Whitman, who was neither a novelist nor a contemporary of his, but a nineteenth-century poet that nonetheless embodied all the aspects of America that early Twentieth-century Italian authors liked the most. Whitman (later the subject of Pavese's graduate thesis) even became an iconic author for the Italian Futurists, for his celebration of the forces of nature, of spontaneity, of impulse, of individualism, of freedom and for his search for the absolute:

> I celebrate myself,
> And what I assume you shall assume,
> For every atom belonging to me as good belongs to you.
> [...]
> I know I am august,
> I do not trouble my spirit to vindicate itself or be understood,
> I see that the elementary laws never apologize,
> I reckon I behave no prouder than the level I plant my
> house by after all.
> [...]
> Divine am I inside and out, and I make holy whatever I touch, or am
> touched from [...]
> (Whitman 1855, 13-56).

As early as 1908 and already seduced by the *Übermensch*, Papini the Futurist wrote:

> From *Leaves of Grass*, a small Nietzschean chrestomathy can easily be extracted, in which even the prophet of Zarathustra's favorite would be found. [...] And not only does he feel, even before Nietzsche, this sense of the virtue of the earth, but also the expectation of a superior race of men (Papini 1908, 704; author's translation).

This very essay also contains more enlightened passages, in which the author briefly drops his *neo-scapigliata* attitude and concentrates on Whitman's literature *per se*. He especially focuses on the spiritual approach of Whitman, who celebrates himself as a human being and, as such, as a sample of nature's creative force, warning that:

> [...] anyone who took this self-worship as decisive proof of Whitman's individualism would be wrong. He worships the self because he worships the whole and sees the whole reflected in himself and feels himself intimately blended in with the whole (Papini 1908, 700; author's translation).

Papini thus seems to really grasp the substance of Whitman's message, giving away, from behind his clownish Futurist mask, his great critical sensitivity. Not much differently from Pavese,[17] he indeed states that "Walt Whitman's personalism is therefore a garment, a peel of his cosmic love for all things. He aspires, like all great souls, to the whole and to infinity, but he does not want to reach it through general and abstract words" (Papini 1908, 701; author's translation).

In the end, Papini gives up to his rebellious impulses and finishes his paper with a very Futurist invitation, which he himself would follow for many years:

> We must go out, get out of the city and feel and love all things directly, the most delicate and the dirtiest, and express our love without regard for anyone, without sweet little words, without metric expedients, without too much respect for holy traditions, honest conventions and stupid rules of high society. We need to become a bit *barbarian* again - maybe a bit *boorish* - if we want to rediscover Poetry. (Papini 1908, 711; author's translation)

This further connotation of the adjective *barbari* (*beceri*, or boorish) supports the conclusion that the liveliness, the freedom and the energy of a 'new' nature and a 'new' culture were what mostly struck the Italian intellectuals of the first half of the Twentieth century about America. In such innocence they discerned a wild aspect, a sort of primitivism that they either rejected (as did the refined art critic Emilio Cecchi) or felt attracted to (Papini, Vittorini, Pavese), either way, hoping that such a 'fury' may prove itself an innovative force for Italian literature, which they perceived as ancient as it was depleted.

In sum, the intellectuals' literary yearnings were integrated by the lower classes' Eldorado vision of America and the hybrid idea that the middle class had of it, more often than not fascinated by the superficial aspects of the country told by the newspapers: jazz, the cinema, the skyscrapers, the continuous output of cars from the tireless assembly lines.[18] The second

---

[17] "All of Walt Whitman's great pages [...] share only one design: the strong, thoughtful, 'receptive' man, who passes through the phenomena of the world and absorbs them all, enraptured by their simplicity, normality, reality, and to these he responds with an attachment, a perennial ecstasy, born of man's fantastic identification with humans and things" (Pavese 1951c, 141; author's translation).

[18] "The experience made [...] begins to interact, in the early years of the century, with new forms of communication and entertainment that overlap with the more purely literary or dramaturgical ones in shaping the image of emigration and of the emigrant" (Franzina 1996, 118; author's translation).

generation of Americanist translators, who include 'Our Mr Pavese',[19] with their choice of authors, contributed to debunk some of these myths (William Faulkner and John Dos Passos tell us that in America too one can suffer), while creating others (Sherwood Anderson, John Steinbeck and Ernest Hemingway reply that in America one may suffer, but one can always pursue one's freedom). Their main achievement remains, however, that of making American literature available to the Italian public, thus starting the first *mass* literary, cultural, and translating phenomenon of Twentieth-century Italy.

4. A chronology of the myth

Earlier on, reference was made to Fernandez's work on the Italian Americanist myth and the role that Pavese and Vittorini had in it. Clearly much more has been written about Cesare Pavese as an author in his own right than as a(n Americanist) translator. Among the studies published about the latter aspect, Fernandez's is one of the most specific, and is frequently cited by those dealing with Pavese's translating activity. The French critic indeed attributes Pavese great importance; he in fact *entirely* identifies the rise and fall of the American myth with Pavese's translating career. In line, among others, with Ferme, thus not fully agreeing with the chronological limits ("ormai [...] anacronistiche": Ferme 2002, 86) that Fernandez proposes, it is suggested here that the very concepts of 'Americanism' and 'American myth' ought to be redefined, in order to correctly place Pavese the translator within them.

According to Fernarndez,

> The myth proper does not begin until November 1930, with Pavese's essay on Sinclair Lewis. It is correct to have the myth start from this date, just as it is correct to have it end twenty years later, in 1950, with the death of Pavese, because there is no doubt that Pavese's personality had a decisive effect on the birth, life, orientation, content of the myth. (Franzina 1996, 11-12; author's translation).

The first clarification to be made here is the definition of *mito americano*. With this term, Fernandez indicates the enthusiasm for contemporary American literature shown by Italian authors between 1930 and 1950, fuelled by the high number of American novels translated in that twenty years, to which Pavese and Vittorini first and significantly contributed. In fact, *mito americano* is a very generic term, commonly used in connection with

---

[19] *Our Mr. Wrenn* by Sinclair Lewis was the first American novel translated by Pavese in 1931 (*Il nostro signor Wrenn. Storia di un gentiluomo romantico*, Firenze, Bemporad).

heterogeneous concepts, persons, and events. These go from the hopes for fabulous fortunes nurtured by the Italians who emigrated to America, to the manufacturing of the first Ford automobiles, to the New Deal that allowed the US economy to rise again, to John F. Kennedy, Marylin Monroe, Coca-Cola, Levi's jeans and much more. Whether real or the result of the fascination exerted on Europe by America, the new continent has been producing all sorts of myths, which continue to rise and fall according to trends and fashions. Based on Fernandez's definition, though, the term *mito americano* shall only refer to the 1930-1950 period, during which American literary works were assiduously translated and the American culture was spread in Italy. The term *americanismo,*[20] on the other hand, interchangeably used by critics to refer to the same concept, shall indicate a more general interest in America, especially of a *literary* kind. Redefined as such, it appears that there was more than just one *americanismo*: Nencioni's *americanismo* was one, Cecchi's was another and Pavese's yet another. Not only, *l'americanismo* in general survived *il mito americano*, since the love of Italians for American literature may have decreased after 1950, but certainly did not altogether cease; it rather changed into the umpteenth form of Americanism.

Moving from this distinction, the beginning of the Twentieth-century Americanism may still be set in the period between 1920-1930, when some partial knowledge of America, filtered through old literary myths (Chateaubriand) and new social and cultural myths (emigrants' fortunes), already existed. From the strict perspective of literary criticism, instead, the Italians' interest in America did possibly emerge with Nencioni and boomed with the first generation of translators and Americanists from the early Twentieth century: Cecchi, Linati, and Praz. As regards the 'American myth' proper, i.e., the time of the young Italian intellectuals' exaltation for their American contemporaries Faulkner, Anderson, Lewis, Saroyan, Lee Masters, Dos Passos, Fitzgerald and for a certain America that they described, it may well be seen to have started, following Fernandez, in 1930, with Pavese's essay on Sinclair Lewis.[21] This study undoubtedly contributed to the foundation of the *mito americano*, this time not based on a social phenomenon, such as emigration, but on a purely literary interest.

Concerning Pavese's specific role, it is worth recalling that 1930 only represented the moment when his own Americanism first became public, as he began writing in *La Cultura*: his love for British and American literature, as is well known, dated back to his secondary-school days. Nor did his translating

---

[20] The term *mitoamericanismo* has also been proposed by Pietropaoli 1988-1990, 555.

[21] About twenty pages, published in *La Cultura* in 1930. See Pavese 1951e, 5.

only begin in 1931: Sinclair Lewis's *Our Mr Wrenn* was the first translation that he published, but Pavese had enjoyed translating on his own from ancient Greek, German, and English ever since he was a student at the Massimo D'Azeglio *liceo*, first, and, then, at university. Attilio Dughera, who researched the young Pavese's work, notes that

> the manuscripts from his youth are truly surprising, for their large number of different literary genres: short stories, critical essays written "in freedom", annotations of various types, translations from German and English. (Dughera 1992, 9; author's translation).

Still, on his translations from ancient Greek, Dughera details Pavese's habit of using English terms when he found them more suitable than Italian ones to render the Greek originals.[22] This naïve method, as well as showing Pavese already knew English when quite young, also proves his concern about the faithful rendering of a text. Thus Pavese, like many other students, learnt to translate as he studied his classics. Differently from others, though, the art or 'trade' (*mestiere*) of translating did not remain for him a mere scholastic exercise but changed into a real passion, also thanks to his encounter with English. This language would enable him to access not only Shakespeare (whom he would always consider a classic, just like Greek and Latin authors), but also the contemporary American writers, whose social protest and lively language and style could not but appeal strongly to his young spirit, still imbued with Romanticism yet already looking for novel suggestions. Therefore, what is proposed here is that Pavese's columns in *La Cultura* and his first published translations are not to be considered the *beginning* of his interest in America but only his formal public emergence as a translator and a writer.[23]

Coming to the end of the myth, a preliminary consideration is necessary. Eighteen translations were published during Pavese's lifetime: 14 novels, an autobiography and three historical essays, distributed between 1931 and

---

[22] "To preserve the unity of the Greek word, Pavese resorts to the aid of other languages, such as Latin [...]. But also English, a language familiar to the writer, often appears with this purpose, although almost always in the same forms (*someway, anyway, somewhere, anywhere* ...). Pavese feels that in this way he translates more faithfully, since with these foreign words he can produce an exact, almost visible transcription" (Dughera 1992, 33-34; author's translation).

[23] 'Writer', here, is to be understood as 'essayist', since his first collection of poems, *Lavorare stanca*, would be published in 1936, and his first novel, *Paesi tuoi*, as late as 1941.

1950.[24] This timespan should actually be reduced to the 11 years comprised between 1931 and 1942, since this was Pavese's actual 'age of translations', in which he published *16 out of 18* – practically all – of them. For this reason, Fernandez's belief that the American myth in Italy coincided and ended with Pavese's literary (and real) life in 1950 appears little defensible. The moments cannot coincide, as Pavese's Americanism was over by 1942 – well before his death in 1950, or even 1947, when he last translated a novel, and which should be considered a tardy epilogue to his translating experience. Apart from Pavese's death, the other reasons that Fernandez gives for setting the end of the American myth in 1950 are, on the contrary, quite understandable. Among them, he mentions, for example, the Vittorini-Togliatti polemic in the magazine *Il Politecnico* (1945-1947), the Italian Communist Party joining the political minority in 1948, the Korean War and the US taking sides against the USSR and China in 1950. All these events contributed to start a crisis in the cultural sensitivity of Italians, and to change their attitude towards America. Once again, though, only one of the American myths ended around 1950: the first literary myth arisen in the 1930s around Anderson, Faulkner, Lee Masters, Fitzgerald, and so on. Since then, the 'American dream' in Italy has had its ups and downs, connected with the US's political positions as a world leader: the Cold War, the Vietnam War, the Iraqi Wars, the 9/11 attacks, and the Barack Obama presidency are only some of the events that alternatively made the American myth rise and fall in the post-war era.

In other words, whereas Pavese's individual Americanism ought to be distinguished from the American myth (itself, in turn, a complex phenomenon), they both need to be placed within the more general literary Americanism. Three different experiences thus occurred between 1930 and 1950, as illustrated in Fig. 4.1.

The figure compares the chronology of three different though connected phenomena: Pavese's Americanism, the American myth, and Americanism in general.

---

[24] To these, the following posthumous translations should be added: Hesiod, Homer, *La teogonia di Esiodo e tre inni omerici*, trans. Cesare Pavese, ed. by Attilio Dughera (Torino: Einaudi, 1981) and Percy. B. Shelley, *Prometeo slegato*, trans. Cesare Pavese, in "Collezione di Poesia", ed. by Mark Pietralunga (Torino: Einaudi, 1997). See Table 4.1.

Figure 4.1

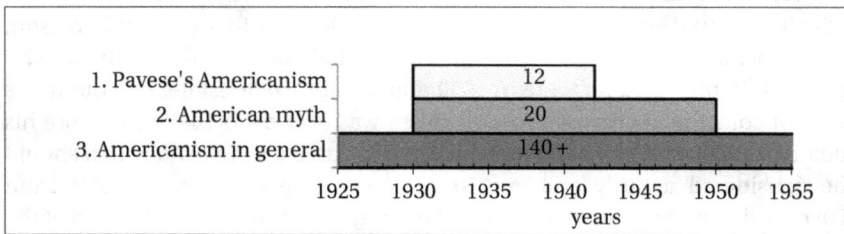

Pavese's Americanism, the American myth, Americanism in general

1) The author Pavese used his 1930-1942 Americanist period to forge his own writing (see Esposito 2018), inspired by the innovations in the contemporary American authors he read and translated. It seems appropriate to identify 1942 as the end of this period of his, because neither the translations nor the essays published after that year were significant either quantitatively or qualitatively, at least from an Americanist viewpoint. Between 1942 and 1950, Pavese only translated two works,[25] both by British authors: a novel by the then-emerging young writer Robert Henriques (1947) and a long essay by the historian Arnold Toynbee (1950).[26] As regards his essays, in that period, he mostly wrote about British authors such as Joseph Conrad and Robert L. Stevenson, while those about America were much less passionate than those he wrote in the 1930s and, in some cases, they even sounded apologetic of (though by no means rejecting it) his juvenile enthusiasm.[27] Finally, his statement

---

[25] Three, if one considers Pavese's version of Hesiod's *Theogony* and three Homeric hymns, which nevertheless have not been considered here, since they were a) translated from ancient Greek and not from English and b) not originally conceived for publication (they first appeared in 1981). See Table 4.1.

[26] Often underestimated or even ignored (even a critic of Fernandez's Pavesian Americanist myth such as Vece, who identifies the peak of Pavese's American interest in Anderson's and Melville's novels, would, perhaps with a hint of naivete, dismiss Pavese's incursion into the complexities of Joyce's *Portrait* as a "breve interruzione per dedicarsi a *Ritratto dell'artista da giovane* di James Joyce nel 1933" (Vece 2002, 136), the fondness of and relevance for Pavese of the British authors he translated ought to be the subject of a major work of its own.

[27] "Italy was estranged, barbaric, calcified – it had to be shaken, decongested and re-exposed to all the spring winds blowing in from Europe and the world. It is no surprise that this act of conquering texts could not be done by bureaucrats or literary laborers, but it took youthful enthusiasm and involvement" (Pavese 1951d, 245; author's translation).

> [*Selezione* is] smoke-and-mirrors for "Americanistic" propaganda. Its subject indeed alternates between the pedantic exaltation of ever new facets of the "American dream" and the condemnation of ever new · inequities of the socialist world. (Pavese 1951a/2014, no page; author's translation).

possibly marks the end of his romance with the American myth and his turn towards the Communist ideals. The last significant episode in Pavese's translating age should therefore be considered his 1942 translation of William Faulkner's *The Hamlet*, after which he would turn to his more mature interests: novel writing and publishing.

2) The beginning of the 'American myth' in Italy can also be set in 1930. However, since Pavese was not the only intellectual who fed it, establishing its end in 1942 does not seem completely accurate, as that was when Pavese *only* ceased to be interested in it. The success and spread of the literature from across the Atlantic in fact continued well after that year, at least – as Fernandez maintains – until 1950. Elio Vittorini, Eugenio Montale, Alberto Rossi, but also Fernanda Pivano, Gabriele Baldini, Agostino Lombardo, Glauco Cambon – whom Fernandez laconically brands "the third generation, that of historians and professors", "scholastic, in spirit and in style" (Fernandez 1969, 112; 111; author's translation) – were still or already or would soon be at work. They and several other Americanists picked up the previous generations' work from where they had left it and created an ideal (or a real, in the case of Pivano, a close friend and partner of Pavese's) connection with the era of the early Americanist enthusiasm and the more mature and better-informed cultural exchange that emerged after the Second World War. Fernandez's reasons, listed above, for choosing the year 1950 all seem valid: it is their order of importance that perhaps needs changing. What he perceives as the main cause of the end of the American myth (Pavese's death) was possibly not so decisive as some political events of the period: the mentioned anti-American cultural turn of the Italian Communist Party (1945-1947) and Vittorini's break with it, the Italian Communist Party becoming a minority party in 1948, the war that split Korea at the thirty-eighth parallel, the US novel opposition to the USSR and China. These, much more than the death of what was, after all, a single translator (no matter how relevant his role in the creation of the myth) probably influenced the public's change of attitude towards American culture. The coincidence of Pavese's death in 1950 with the waning of the American myth therefore seems accidental, for at least two different reasons. Firstly, American culture had at that time become independent of Pavese's single-handed work, and enjoyed the support of many other translators, intellectuals, and readers. Secondly, the political climate full of suspicion that would soon give rise to the Cold War had already started to affect the Italian pre-war enthusiasm for legendary America.

Rather than the Eldorado of the early Italian migrants, it now appeared as a military power way too strong for both its enemies and allies alike. The synchronous disappearance of Pavese and of the American myth he had 'fathered' ought to be seen as a mere – though a highly symbolic – coincidence: the myth he had forged had long since left his translating workshop and become independent of him; similarly, it ended without his being responsible for it.

3) Finally, Americanism as a general concept, meant as the study of American literature, had started in Italy long before 1930, with earlier translators and critics, and continued, with later translators and critics, well after 1942 or 1950. Both Pavese's Americanism and the twenty-year 'American myth' should be placed within this wider phenomenon. Thus, maintaining that 'Americanism' began and ended with Pavese and Vittorini is only acceptable if it means the spread of certain American writers, arbitrarily chosen according to the tastes of just two Americanists, and not even experts at that but merely enthusiastic 'amateurs'. Such clarifications seem necessary in order to both downsize the linguistic relevance of their translations, often and inaccurately considered always impeccable, but to similarly keep celebrating, after seventy years, the extraordinary and undiminished cultural value of their Americanist activism. After World War II, the Italian publishing industry, also encouraged by their successful cultural operation, significantly invested in translations, and the Italian public could eventually get a better, wider idea of American fiction.[28] Additionally, there also started to emerge and flourish a great number of academic studies on American literature – for the first time seen as a subject in its own right and not as a mere 'branch' of its British counterpart. Since then, America has been successful with both popular and academic publishers.

Perspectives closer to the one proposed here, i.e., a re-positioning and a re-shaping of the role of Pavese's translations within the Italian *americanismo*, have started to emerge as prevalent (perhaps expectedly and anyway long due[29]) over the first couple of decades of this century – see, e.g., Pino Fasano's view that "that America is not real [Pavese's] contemporary America" but "an existential not [… a] literary model," so that "America is the search for lost Italy" (Fasano 2008, 297; 306). Also recently, Roberto Ludovico has confirmed that

---

[28] An outstanding example is that of the great publisher Arnoldo Mondadori who, in 1945, "having recovered the large presses that had ended up beyond the Iron Curtain, and having obtained a big loan from the Americans to rebuild the plant, [...] began the recovery by printing millions of copies a month of magazines and paperbacks for foreign clients, from «Selezione del Reader's Digest» to «Collins» and «Albatros»" (Ragone 1999, 174; author's translation).

[29] See Rimanelli 2019.

Pavese's *americanismo*, just like publisher Franco Antonicelli's, might rather have been a sort of "ideal Europeism" (Ludovico 2011, 319). What is indisputable is that the blend of 'high' and 'low' culture that is taken for granted these days could not have been possible, in Italy, without the enthusiastic and reckless 'American decade' of Pavese, Vittorini & co. – with the caveat that this legendary decade was Pavese's own wording from as late as 1946 (Pavese 1951d, 247) and, as such, might as well be a myth (un)consciously evoked by an intellectual whose literal statements should always be weighed against his masterful skill and love for myth creation.

Bibliography

Billiani, F. (2007). *Culture nazionali e migrazioni straniere. Italia, 1903-1943*. Firenze: Le Lettere

Cartasegna, M. (1952). "Influenza degli scrittori americani sulla narrativa italiana", *Studium*, VII-VIII, July-August, pp. 429-434

Dughera, A. (1992). *Tra le carte di Pavese*. Roma: Bulzoni

Dunnett, J. (2015). *The 'Mito Americano' and Italian Literary Culture under Fascism*. Ariccia: Aracne

Esposito, E. (2018). *Con altra voce. La traduzione letteraria tra le due guerre*. Roma: Donzelli

Fasano, P. (2008) "Il mito americano di Cesare Pavese", *Italica*, 85(2-3), Summer-Autumn, pp. 295-310

Ferme, V. (2002). *Tradurre è tradire. La traduzione come sovversione culturale sotto il fascismo*. Ravenna: Longo

Fernandez, D. (1969). *Il mito dell'America negli intellettuali italiani dal 1930 al 1950*, translated by A. Zaccaria. Caltanissetta-Roma: Sciascia

Franzina, E. (1996). *Dall'Arcadia in America*. Torino: Edizioni della Fondazione Giovanni Agnelli

Guglielmi, M. (1995). "La letteratura americana tradotta in Italia nel decennio 1930-1940: Vittorini e l'antologia *Americana*", *Forum Italicum: A Journal of Italian Studies*, 29(2), September, pp. 301-312

Haines, M. R. (2000). "French migration to the United States: 1820 to 1950", *Annales de Démographie Historique*, 1, pp. 77-91

Lombardo, A. (1961). *La ricerca del vero*. Roma: Edizioni di storia e letteratura

Ludovico, R. (2011). "Franco Antonicelli e Cesare Pavese", *Italica*, 88(3), Autumn, pp. 317-334

Mesiano, L. (2007). *Cesare Pavese di carta e di parole. Bibliografia ragionata e analitica*. Alessandria: Edizioni dell'Orso

Papini, G. (1908). "Walt Whitman", *Nuova Antologia*, CCXIX(135), May-June, pp. 696-711

Pavese, C. (1951a/2014). *Cultura democratica e cultura americana*, in Pavese, C. *La letteratura americana e altri saggi*, edited by I. Calvino. Torino: Einaudi, electronic version

—————— (1951b). *Ieri e oggi*, in Pavese, C. *La letteratura americana e altri saggi*, edited by I. Calvino. Torino: Einaudi, pp. 193-196

—————— (1951c). *Poesia del far poesia*, in Pavese, C. *La letteratura americana e altri saggi*, edited by I. Calvino. Torino: Einaudi, pp. 141-165

—————— (1951d). *L'influsso degli eventi*, in Pavese, C. *La letteratura americana e altri saggi*, edited by I. Calvino. Torino: Einaudi, pp. 245-248

—————— (1951e). *Senza provinciali, una letteratura non ha nerbo*, in Pavese, C. *La letteratura americana e altri saggi*, edited by I. Calvino. Torino: Einaudi, pp. 9-31

Pietralunga, M. (2005). *Il mito di una scoperta: Pavese traduce* Passage to India *di Walt Whitman*, in Campanello, M. (ed.). *Cesare Pavese. Atti del Convegno internazionale di studi*. Firenze: Olschki, pp. 111-129

Pietropaoli, A. (1988-1990). *La storia del mito d'America in Pavese*, in Rena, L. (ed.). *Humanitas e poesia: studi in onore di Gioacchino Paparelli*. Salerno: Laveglia, pp. 555-569

Prezzolini, G. (1958a). *Perché l'America non capisce l'Europa*, in Prezzolini, G. *Tutta l'America*. Firenze: Vallecchi, pp. 45-53

—————— (1958b). *Tre pregiudizi italiani sull'America*, in Prezzolini, G. *Tutta l'America*. Firenze: Vallecchi, pp. 29-33

Ragone, G. (1999). *Un secolo di libri: storia dell'editoria in Italia dall'Unità al post-moderno*. Torino: Einaudi

Vittorini, E. (ed.). (1941). *Americana. Raccolta di narratori dalle origini ai nostri giorni*. Milano: Bompiani

Whitman, W. (1855). *Song of Myself*, in Whitman, W. *Leaves of Grass*. Brooklyn: Rome Brothers, pp. 13-56

Further Reading

Carducci, N. (1973). *Gli intellettuali e l'ideologia americana*. Manduria: Lacaita

Montale, E. (1939). *Le occasioni*. Torino: Einaudi

Rimanelli, G. (2019). *Cesare Pavese's Long Journey: A Critical-Analytical Study*, edited by M. Pietralunga. New York: Bordighera Press

Sapiro, G. (2016). "Faulkner in France", *Journal of World Literature*, 1(3), 391-411

Walford-Dellù, M. (2015). *Pavese e la critica (1941-2000)*. PhD dissertation, University of Chicago

Chapter 5

Learning from the Past:
Cesare Pavese's First Steps with the
American Publishing World

Mark Pietralunga
Florida State University

Abstract

This essay examines the interest and promotion of Cesare Pavese's works in the United States, with particular focus on the immediate postwar years up to the 1960s. It explores the editorial process regarding Pavese's writings, the "American" perspective of the Piedmontese writer's works and contemporary Italian literature in general as well as the tastes of the American reading public. The essay also addresses questions concerning the negotiations and quality of translations from Italian into English and how such issues may have impacted, up to the present, the publication and reception of Pavese's works in the United States. By contributing to a greater awareness of the publishing obstacles and challenges Pavese's writings met in the early years, this essay seeks to build on and expand the Piedmontese author's critical and popular recognition among an English-speaking readership.

Keywords: Cesare Pavese; Alfred A. Knopf Publishing Company; Sanford J. Greenburger; Giulio Einaudi Editore; Italo Calvino; Tim Parks

* * *

Lawrence G. Smith, the author of the critically acclaimed study, *Cesare Pavese and America*, shared with me a few years ago the following observation concerning the fortune of Pavese's works in America: "I've always contended that one of the reasons Pavese is not well-known in America is the quality of the translations of his novels and short stories. Those translations range from the barely competent to the truly terrible. He [Pavese] has had much better luck with his poetry, essays, and *Dialoghi con Leucò.*"[1] With this observation in mind, it struck me as appropriate to revisit the reception of Pavese's works by the American publishing world in the early years and to consider questions concerning the negotiations and quality of translations from Italian into English raised by publishers and critics and how such issues may have resulted in the Piedmontese writer not achieving a more widespread success. In doing so, I have chosen to focus on the correspondence related to Pavese's works found in the collection of the prestigious Alfred A. Knopf publishing firm at the Harry Ransom Center of the University of Texas at Austin and among the papers of the literary agent and book scout Sanford J. Greenburger at the University of Oregon Libraries Special Collections and University Archives.

Before we turn our attention to the above-mentioned correspondence, we might briefly consider the translation and publication of Italian literature into English, particularly in those years that Pavese's works began circulating among American publishers. An important point to address in this context is the quality of translations into English. In the preface to his 1968 volume *Three Italian Novelists: Moravia, Pavese, and Vittorini*, Donald Heiney states that one of the reasons he chose to translate all the excerpts in his study was that "in some cases the authors have been wretchedly translated" (Heiney 1968, x). He adds that "translation is terribly hard work and rather badly paid, and in order to translate a novel adequately, it is necessary for the translator not only to be an expert linguist, but to have something like a novelist's talent in his own right" (Heiney 1968, x). In a letter of October 4th, 1964, to Pavese biographer Davide Lajolo, William Arrowsmith, the translator of *Dialoghi con Leucò* and *Lavorare Stanca*, reinforces Heiney's observations when he refers to the unfortunate quality of Pavese's translations into English and how British and American publishers handle the Piedmontese writer's works:

> Pavese, by the way, has suffered enormously in English translation. The British publisher, Peter Owen, persists in bringing out versions which are infelicitous in the extreme – clumsy, heavy, stilted English prose, without a trace of Pavese's virtues – and copyright law, of course, products [sic] these wretched versions from competition. In America, it is just as bad, if not worse, since the publishers simply import Owen's versions and republish them. It was for this reason that my collaborator, DS Carne-Ross, and I spent most of a year working on the Dialogues.

---

[1] Smith's observation was included in an email dated February 13th, 2019.

Whether we were successful is of course open to question, but I think we made every effort to create an English Pavese as eloquent and forceful as the Italian Pavese.[2]

Over the years, other critics have referred to Pavese's translations as "serviceably enough" (Cambon 1977, 1), "not so much technically bad as *critically* wrong" (Fiedler 1954, 536), "hasty workmanship" (Casson 1965, 25), and "so full of errors as to be unreliable" (Smith 2010, 169).

A helpful resource in addressing the question of quality of translations and how publishing houses handle this product is the 1982 Italian Book and American Publishing conference, held at the American Academy in Rome. A constant theme of the speakers and discussants at the conference was the difficulty of negotiations for the sale or purchase of literary rights, of securing funding for the translations, and of actually getting the resulting translations published. Marco Polillo, then editorial director of the Mondadori Publishing House, spoke of the difficulty of funding translations for the American market. Polillo noted that it was clear from his dealings with the financing of a translation that these types of projects were considered by American publishers to be "a true luxury." He then asks the following key question: "Why is the problem of the translation so much more important in America?" Unlike in Italy where there are "too many good translators," Polillo states that it is very complicated to translate a book from Italian into English because "few native Americans know Italian, and even fewer can handle the onerous task of translating" (Lihua and MacShane 1986, 77-78).

Following up on this point, Robin Healey, in the introduction to her book *Twentieth-Century Italian Literature in Translation: An Annotated Bibliography 1929-1997*, observes that "in Italy, many of the most popular or highly critically regarded writers also prepare and publish in English, and the work of the translation of literature in English is spread among a pool of translators who are also accomplished writers" (Healey 1998, xix). Healey adds that in the English-speaking world, in contrast, a few prolific translators from Italian have among them translated hundreds of books, while the remaining hundreds of translators have only one or a few volumes each to their credit.[3]

During his lifetime and at the time of his death in 1950, no work by Pavese was translated into English. In a January 1951 piece for the *New York Review of Books* treating the contemporary literary landscape in Italy, Paolo Milano

---

[2] The letter is found in the Lajolo Archives in Vinchio d'Asti.

[3] In an interview with L. Venuti, W. Weaver notes that many publishers "regard translators simply as hired help." See Venuti 1982, 24.

introduces Pavese in the following terms: "Cesare Pavese, in many ways the most promising of the new Italian writers and the only significant one still unknown to the American reader killed himself in the fall" (Milano 1951, 28). In an essay treating the Italian literary landscape in America between 1942 and 1952, Dante Della Terza refers to a "letter" from Italy written by translator and critic D. D. Paige and addressed to editor Louis Brigante, who published it in his review *Intro* (Della Terza 2001, 104-105). In the 'letter,' Paige asserts that, despite its general high level, the contemporary Italian narrative "doesn't travel well." Paige adds that the American, or the Frenchman for that matter, "becomes impatient: Italian writing is for him too parochial in an age in which literature becomes increasingly international" (Paige 1952, 21). Paige holds firm to the opinion that contemporary Italian literature is either boring, lacks an experimental capacity, or finds itself lost among seemingly disparate linguistic options: a lofty, archaic, and strictly literary vocabulary or colloquial and vernacular style. Among those authors spared by Paige "from folkloristic debris and from purely internal consumption," writes Della Terza, is Pavese, despite his so-called "lapses into slang or for his lofty literary longings" (Della Terza 2001, 104). Della Terza appears to sympathize with Paige's "criticism" of Pavese's style on the grounds of a tension that emerges between the translator of *Tra donne sole* and *Il diavolo sulle colline* and their author in tackling the "impervious barrier of analogies, anacoluthons, and derisive strikes against the national linguistic *koine* on one hand and the sophisticated choices that the narrative circumstances suggested on the other." These choices, continues Della Terza, appeared, at the lexical level, to conflict with the "tone of fragmentation and stylistic *sprezzatura* that the dialogue of the narrative assumed in Pavese" (Della Terza 2001, 105).

In his introduction to *The Moon and the Bonfires*, the first work of Pavese's to be published into English,[4] Paolo Milano's question of why the delay in translating the Piedmontese writer's works seems to fit with the difficulties Della Terza identifies above:

Whenever I have found myself with an Italian friend, discussing the lively interest of Americans in contemporary Italian fiction – in the work of Alberto Moravia, Carlo Levi, Vasco Pratolini, Giuseppe Berto, Elio Vittorini, Elsa Morante, and the rest – invariably I have been asked, "Why hasn't Pavese been translated yet?" A natural enough question, because Italians consider Pavese's novelettes to be the finest, if not the most colorful, fruit of the postwar literary crop. "Of course," my Italian

---

[4] The first English translation of *La luna e i falò* was by L. Sinclair and was published by the John Lehman Limited publishing house in 1952.

friends usually add, "how could Pavese's elliptic and allusive style bear translation of any kind?" (Milano 1951, vii)

Despite Leslie Fiedler's championing Pavese in his pioneering 1954 article in *The Kenyon Review* titled "Introducing Cesare Pavese," Frances Keene, in her introduction to the English translation of Pavese's diary *Il mestiere di vivere* which appeared several years later in 1961, speaks to a general unfamiliarity with the Piedmontese writer's life and works in the United States:

> [...] in this country Pavese's novels have been published haphazardly and the myth of his personality has been imperfectly documented. In Italy and France he is, with Elio Vittorini and Alberto Moravia, established in the front rank of contemporary Italian authors, and he is read increasingly in England. We have yet to have a coherent view of Pavese in the United States, and the publication of this journal should be a step in that direction. (Pavese 1961, 7)

While the publication of Pavese's diary was a step in the right direction in providing a more "coherent view" of the writer, Stanley Edgar Hyman, as late as 1968, would write in his review of R. W. Flint's edition *The Selected Novels of Cesare Pavese* that "Cesare Pavese is still not very well known in this country, but he is the most prominent postwar novelist" (Hyman 1968, 114). In the same year of the publication of his edition of Pavese's novels, R. W. Flint published the essay *Translating Cesare Pavese* in which he explored in detail the question of why such quality as Pavese's writings had to wait so long for recognition outside of Italy. In his essay, Flint reflects on the versions of the early translators: "The first translators, all presumably young men, had overlaid the text with often amusing, sometimes hilarious, record of breezy enthusiasm, snuffy timidities, and general miscomprehension with which the Anglo-American world had first greeted a prostrate Italy when the war was over" (Flint 1968, 156). Flint is quick to point out that these early translators "were not equally or uniformly bad"; however, what appeared unsettling to them was "Pavese's novel combination of gentility and profanity, mildness and rigor, saturnine subversive humor and high poetic elevation" (Flint 1968, 157).

1. Alfred A. Knopf Publishing Company and Cesare Pavese

The Alfred A. Knopf Publishing Company's interest in Pavese dates back to 1948. In a letter of July 22nd, 1948, the secretary to Harold Strauss, the publishing firm's editor-in-chief, writes literary agent Sanford J. Greenburger expressing an interest in seeing a copy of the Italian author's new novel,

Memorie di due stagioni.[5] The description below of the forthcoming work by one of Knopf's consultants was based on an Einaudi promotional release:

> A new novel by Cesare Pavese, *Memorie di due stagioni.* Pavese is a very able writer of the proletarian (in fact, Communist) school, who also copies American techniques and is known as a translator of American books. One of his novels, *Paesi tuoi*, was recently translated into French. His political views are not crude, but subtle, and he knows how to write.[6]

There are no further records in the Knopf collection related to the initial interest in the novel. However, just a few days following the inquiry about *Memorie di due stagioni*, Blanche Knopf, Alfred's wife and an important presence in the publishing company, writes President Luigi Einaudi on August 4th, 1948, informing him that she had recently seen his son Mario Einaudi, who was a representative for his brother's publishing firm in the United States as well as a professor in the Department of Government at Cornell University, and expresses her interest in meeting the Italian leader during her upcoming trip to Rome later that month "to find new authors to translate and publish in this country as well as meeting some of the publishers whom we have been in contact over the years."[7]

In the Einaudi Archive in Turin, one finds correspondence between Giulio Einaudi and Blanche Knopf, not long after the latter's visit to Italy, that refers to the publication of Pavese's two novelette volume *Prima che il gallo canti*. In a letter of January 22nd, 1949, Einaudi writes to Blanche Knopf, in an awkwardly constructed English, and points out the success of the recent publication: "As for our books we think particularly interesting for you we suggest you would ask Greenburger for 'Prima che il gallo canti' Pavese's latest book, which is getting a very big success in Italy."[8] An interest in Pavese's most recent book is shared by one of Knopf's internal readers in a report on the publication of the *Antologia Einaudi 1948* dated March 1949.[9] In the report, the consultant mentions a familiarity with some of the Italian authors highlighted in the

---

[5] The letter is located in Folder 29.6 of the Knopf Collection. *Memorie di due Stagioni* was the original title of the story that was later published as *Il carcere.*

[6] The report is signed "FFL" and is located in Folder 29.6.

[7] The letter is found in Folder 31.6 of the Knopf Collection. Much of the material in this folder is related to Blanche Knopf's trip to Italy.

[8] The letter is found in the Mario Einaudi Folder at the State Archive of Turin-Einaudi Archive.

[9] The report is found in Folder 47.1 and is signed FFL.

Anthology, including Pavese, and suggests that *Prima che il gallo canti* be given special attention by the publishing firm: "Pavese is brutal and difficult but alive – his form is American, his subjects often by implication Communistic. He has a new book coming out *Prima che il gallo canti* (Before the Cock Crows), which ought to be looked at."[10]

Notwithstanding the publishing house's interest, Blanche Knopf, in a letter of May 31st, 1949, informs Einaudi of the decision not to publish the Pavese volume, despite her continued interest in the author:

> Dear Sr. Einaudi,
> I have given a great deal of thought to Cesare Pavese's *Prima che il gallo canti* and I am afraid it is not a book that we can publish. It is split in two and is not at all right, in my opinion, for this market. Pavese, of course, I am interested in and hope that we can get a novel that we can undertake from him at some future time.[11]

In his response to Mrs. Knopf on June 19th, 1949, Einaudi reaffirms the success that *Prima che il gallo canti* had in Italy and adds that "apparently Italian and American readers have not the same taste at all."[12] Despite Knopf's decision not to publish *Prima che il gallo canti*, the publishing house continued to show an interest in the work. In a letter of September 19th, 1950, Wayne Kerwood, the personal assistant to Blanche Knopf, writes Greenburger inquiring about the status of *Prima che il gallo canti* and *La luna e i falò*.[13]

It is not until April of 1960 that we find Pavese's works mentioned again in the Knopf correspondence. In a brief memo dated April 4th, 1960, from Blanche Knopf to translator and editor Sophie Wilkins, we find a list of Pavese's works that had been published in English in the United States, along with those that appeared in England or Canada:

> Published in the U.S.
> *Devil in the Hills*. 1960, Noonday, $1.25 tr. D.D. Paige
> *Moon and the Bonfires*. 1953, Farrar & Straus, tr. Marianne Ceconi $3.00 forward Paolo Milano, (also tr. Louise Sinclair, 1952) Published Toronto, London.

---

[10] *Ibid.*

[11] The letter is found in the Mario Einaudi Folder at the State Archive in Turin-Einaudi Archive.

[12] *Ibid.*

[13] The letter is found in Folder 67.5 of the Knopf Collection.

(Other publications in English, by Wen, London or Toronto, *The House on the Hill,* '56, the *Political Prisoner,* with *The Beautiful Summer, Among Women Only* (1953, Owen) price given in shillings and pence.)[14]

Over the years, Italo Calvino figures prominently in the Einaudi-Knopf correspondence both as a writer and as a consultant for the Turin publishing firm. In his latter role, Calvino explored with Knopf those Italian authors who published with Einaudi and who could be of interest to an American public. One of the authors was Cesare Pavese. In a letter of November 22nd, 1959, written shortly after his arrival in the United States on a Ford Foundation grant, Calvino shares his thoughts on the American publishing industry with Giulio Einaudi and his wife Renata. Despite establishing as a rule of thumb upon his arrival in the United States not to take on the traditional anti-American point of view, disputing issues related to industrial mass culture, Calvino admits to being struck by the manner in which the American publishers consider literature in their everyday practices: "All show that general lack of personality, of ingenuity, that we have heard so many complaints about the theory, and when you find yourself surrounded by this day after day, at a certain point you suddenly feel suffocated by it, as it were" (Calvino 2013, 169). Comparing the American publishers' efficiency with the Italian's lack of organizational skills, Calvino observes that in America "the publishers do not have a soul (or they have a false soul, like the Catholic soul behind Pantheon books), they are purely commercial organizations." Calvino notes that the biggest economy is made on translation: "They don't decide to translate a book (here one lives practically in a regime of publishing autonomy) unless they are sure the costs can be shared with the British publisher" (Calvino 2013, 170). Calvino adds that the publishing houses employ the most rudimentary criteria in their handling of their European production:

> The readers of It.[alian] books for instance are either any editor that happens to know Italian or some poor souls, almost unheard of, so nobody ever knows what to make of their opinions, and publishers go ahead haphazardly, the choice of a book always comes about by chance; and note that it is not just Italian books that this happens to, but also French books which are often read by the same readers; but the idea never crosses their mind that one could choose major specialists as consultants for each country's literature. (Calvino 2013, 170)

---

[14] The memo is found in Folder 295.4 of the Knopf Collection.

Blanche Knopf's letter to Calvino on July 7th, 1961, confirms the American publishing company's continued interest in Pavese. She refers to their many discussions concerning the publishing of Pavese's work and special attention is paid to Einaudi's recent publication of the Italian writer's diary *Il mestiere di vivere*:

> You and I have talked endlessly about the possibility of publishing Pavese's work. Now I understand that you have published his diaries, and I understand that Peter Owen has just published them in London. I am, of course, writing to him, but I imagine that you'll hold the U.S. rights. I would, I repeat, like to reconsider the whole question of translating and publishing Pavese. If you could send me his books together with his diary, I think we could come to a quick decision. As I recall, the books are not very long. In sending them, perhaps you would indicate which ones you consider to be the most important. My best regard to Julio [sic] Einaudi, and to you.[15]

Just a few days later, on July 10th, 1961, Blanche Knopf sends a memo to her assistant Grace Dadd, asking that she look into the rights of Pavese's diary which, as noted above, had recently been published by Peter Owen.[16] Knopf points out the "rave review" that it received by Alfred J. Toynbee in the *Times Literary Supplement*.[17] Although the rights of the diary had already been sold to Walker and Company Publishers, a young editor at Knopf, Howard Fertig,[18] had been given the charge to assess the English translation of the diary, whose title was *The Burning Brand*. In his detailed and enlightening report of November 21st, 1961, Fertig begins by pointing to the "unfailingly intelligent entries" in the diary as a reflection of "the central preoccupations of a man who was, clearly, both an authentic writer and, at his very soul, a suicide." While

---

[15] The letter is found in Folder 327.10 of the Knopf Collection.

[16] The first English translation of the diary by A. E. Murch appeared in England under the title *This Business of Living. Diaries 1935-1950* (London: Peter Owen, 1961), while in the United States it was published with the title *The Burning Brand. Diaries 1935-1950* (New York: Walker and Company Publishers, 1961). Although the titles are different, it is the same translation.

[17] B. Knopf appears to be referring to the Toynbee piece, "A Man and His Novels," published in the *Times Literary Supplement* on the September 15th, 1961. However, there is a discrepancy with dates, since Knopf's memo to Dadd was written two months before the Toynbee review.

[18] H. Fertig founded in 1966 Howard Fertig Publisher. The firm publishes important titles in European History, Literature, and Social Thought. Its titles include works by G. D'Annunzio and L. Pirandello.

recognizing Pavese's "wholly admirable intellect" that always seeks "to objectify private impressions into general principles" and thus modify "the narcissism implicit in diaries," Fertig notes that there still is "an incapable sense of entrapment within the fairly unchanging bounds of his concerns." He is also struck by the fact that "never is there, in all these pages, what one might call a cry – a sound – from out the street," thus leading him to posit that Pavese represents "the case of an introvert seeking salvation through objectivity – externality – and, of course, as his suicide suggests, failing." Fertig asks how else can one interpret that writer "whose journals for the years 1939-1949 (at least insofar as they are presented here) literally never once mention the war, Fascism, the German occupation?" He then adds that this is not said in denigration of his talent but only "to mark the limits of the mode." What stands out as "first-rate" for Fertig is the "literary criticism presented in the book, ranging from extended analyses of Pavese's own work and esthetic aims to discussions of the Greek dramatists and current American novelists." Fertig's concluding remarks also highlight the general lack of familiarity of Pavese's works at this time:

> Granting, then, the quality of Pavese's mind – a quality I am willing to celebrate without qualification – these diaries make for the sort of book to which each reader responds on the basis of his own capacity for indulgence and sympathy. My own, I suspect, would have been increased by a knowledge of Pavese's work and some sense of his achievement as an artist – always an important consideration, I think, in approaching the diary of a writer.[19]

On the same date she receives Fertig's extensive report, Blanche Knopf responds accordingly: "Many thanks for reading the Pavese. It sounds like the book that I should have had and was trying to get when young Mr. Kirk told me he had it. Pavese wrote some fine novels but not saleable – he is dead as you know. I am grateful that you read it."[20] In reflecting on his comments over fifty years after they were written, Fertig recalls: "I, of course, read as one hypnotized my report on Pavese's *Burning Brand,* and no less so Mrs. Knopf's note to me. Though I do not remember the actual circumstances now, rereading these brings back distinct traces of recognition and discovery."[21]

---

[19] The report is found in Folder 327.10 of the Knopf Collection.

[20] *Ibid.*

[21] Fertig's email to me is dated February 8th, 2014.

2. Sanford J. Greenburger Correspondence and Cesare Pavese

To help us frame the documents concerning Pavese in the Greenburger collection at the University of Oregon Libraries, let us first consider relevant correspondence found in the Einaudi Archives at the State Archive of Turin, some of which appeared in the Einaudi publication of Pavese's letters.[22] Additionally, Luisa Mangoni's *Pensare i libri. La casa editrice Einaudi dagli anni trenta agli anni sessanta* offers insightful guidance in navigating the Einaudi Archives and in understanding Greenburger's relations with Einaudi Publishers. In a letter dated February 4th, 1944, Greenburger writes Mario Einaudi and informs him that, after confirming the antifascist nature of the Turin publishing firm, he will act as its exclusive American purchasing agent. Later that year, in a letter to his brother on November 10th, 1944, Mario Einaudi refers to Greenburger's notable ability as a literary agent and his value in building the reputation of Einaudi Publishers in the United States.[23] Despite Mario Einaudi's very positive words to his brother about Greenburger, Pavese, in his role as editor, expresses his reservations concerning the American literary agent in a letter to Giulio Einaudi dated March 27th, 1946.[24] Pavese shares with Einaudi that his contacts at the United States Information Service (USIS) were surprised to hear of the firm's dealings with the American literary agent, given his questionable actions regarding the compensation of authors, and suggests that the publishing firm be more cautious in its dealings with Greenburger. As additional correspondence indicates, Greenburger's role as a literary agent was progressively supplanted by Erich Linder's Milan-based Agenzia Letteraria Internazionale.[25] Despite the concerns and the changes in its talent scouts and literary agents, the collaboration between Einaudi Editore and Greenburger remained a resource and point of reference for the Turin publishing firm for several more years.[26]

---

[22] See Pavese 1966.

[23] The letter is found in the Mario Einaudi Folder at the State Archive of Turin-Einaudi Archive.

[24] The letter is found in the Cesare Pavese Folder at the State Archive of Turin-Einaudi Archive.

[25] In her study, Mangoni traces the reasons for the eventual replacement of Greenburger, which was based primarily on philosophical differences of what constitutes an "Einaudi book" (Mangoni 1999, 459-461).

[26] In a letter of March 9th, 1950, Giulio Einaudi writes his brother Mario after a meeting with Greenburger during the latter's trip to Italy that left him cautiously optimistic in his dealings with the American literary agent: "Il Greenburger mi ha fatto una impressione migliore che al primo incontro di anni fa, e direi che il meglio sia lasciar maturare le cose, seguendolo con attenzione" [My impression of Greenburger was much better than our

In reviewing the sixty items pertaining to Pavese in the Greenburger Collection, one notes that a large portion of the correspondence, which covers the period between 1948 to 1955, focuses on the marketing of the writer's works that were actively promoted by the literary agent among American publishers. An example of the spirit with which Greenburger promoted Pavese's books is captured in his letter to Giulio Einaudi dated January 29th, 1949: "I am looking forward to the reviews of Pavese's new book.[27] I am just as anxious as you are to get Pavese published in America and we have not relented for a moment in our efforts to do so."[28] And in a subsequent letter to Einaudi on February 21st, 1949, Greenburger speaks of urgency and the timeliness of publishing Pavese in America: "We got the reviews of the Pavese book. But we have not yet received a copy of the book. Mischa [sic] wants to read it,[29] and I want to read it because I think the time is ripe for me to get Pavese published in America. So you better send me some copies quick." The correspondence also demonstrates some of the technical and practical questions related to the internal readings of Pavese's works as well as the tastes of the American public. In March and April of 1948, Greenburger exchanges a series of letters with Farrar, Straus and Company concerning the promotion of *Dialoghi con Leucò*, *Il compagno*, and *Paesi tuoi*. Farrar, Straus and Company was particularly interested in receiving reading copies of the latter two works. With regard to *Il compagno*, publisher Roger Straus informs Greenburger in a letter dated April 1st, 1948, of his publishing firm's decision not to publish the work: "After all the fuss and furor, we've decided against the Pavese book, *IL COMPAGNO*, and I'm returning it herewith. It is very interesting, and we've had a good report on it, but I'm afraid it just wouldn't fit into our list." Included among the items in the Greenburger collection is a lengthy reader's report of *Il compagno*, which provides an interesting "American" perspective of Pavese's novel and of contemporary literature in general. Before discussing in detail the novel's plot, the reader

---

first meeting years ago, and I'd say it's better to let things mature and keep a close eye on him]. The letter is found in the Sanford J. Greenburger Folder at the State Archive of Turin-Einaudi Archive.

[27] The book mentioned here and in the subsequent letter is *Prima che il gallo canti*.

[28] Sanford J. Greenburger Literary Agency Records, 1921-1977, Box 13. Unless otherwise stated, all subsequent letters cited from the Greenburger correspondence are found in Box 13.

[29] Mikhail ("Misha") Kamenetzki, who, as a foreign correspondent in the U.S. for *Corriere della sera*, adopted the pen-name Ugo Stille. An Einaudi memorandum, dated September 5, 1945, states that Kamenetzki was authorized by Giulio Einaudi to negotiate book's publishing rights that were of interest to the Einaudi Publishing Firm and was instructed to talk about it with Greenburger. The memorandum is located in the Greenburger Folder of at the State Archive of Turin-Einaudi Archive.

introduces the work as "another novel of the new and lively Italian 'proletarian' school (Vittorini, Pratolini et al.)" and indicates how the author, "who is also a translator of American books, shows in his form and style a strong influence of Hemingway, Caine [sic] and the American realistic writers." From the onset, the reader's report makes clear that the novel has a "definite political slant." However, it emphasizes that the political point "is made with a light and pleasing touch, unlike the heavy-handed manner of Communist writers of other nations." Within the context of "Italian books," Pavese's novel is seen as "notable for its simple colloquial style and its short, slangy sentences, with the repetition between question and answer picked up by Hemingway as a reflection of the way simple people talk." The report also finds the novel's local color excellent, "in its description of small-bit actors, models, truck-drivers and mechanics and the round of amusements of their class: dancing and wine and motorcycles (where in America it would be whiskey and automobiles)." The report describes the novel as "artfully naïve" in its portrayal of "the awakening of political consciousness in a boy with only slightly more sensibility than his fellows," and in its "mingled hard-boiled and sentimental treatment of his love affairs." Despite enjoying the book for "its clipped emphatic style and its local color of a strictly non-picturesque, realistic kind" and for its tone that recalls the film *Open City* "in its ease and naturalness," the reader ultimately concludes that the novel is "untimely, both because of its Communist slant and because it treats the period 1936-37, which events have now outdistanced."

Notwithstanding Farrar, Straus and Company's refusal of *Il compagno*, Greenburger continued to promote it aggressively, believing it to be a good book with which to launch Pavese in the United States. The same could be said for Pavese's novel *Paesi tuoi*, which was turned down by several publishing firms during the same period. On April 15th, 1948, Margaret Wheeler, secretary at Farrar, Straus and Company, returns *Paesi tuoi* and informs Greenburger that, based on a reader's report, they did not think "it would appeal sufficiently to the American public." Nevertheless, the publishing firm remained interested in Pavese and asked Greenburger to keep them advised "as to Pavese's next book, if any, as he is a good writer" and they wanted to keep track of him. Following the refusal of Pavese's books on the part of Farrar, Straus and Company, Greenburger contacted Rutgers University Press about their possible interest in *Dialoghi con Leucò* and Little, Brown and Company concerning *Feria d'agosto* and *Paesi tuoi*. Additionally, Greenburger urged Pellegrini & Cudahy to come to a decision regarding *Il compagno* after they had been considering the novel for several months. For two of the above publishers, Rutgers University Press and Little, Brown and Company, issues related to translation complicated the review process. In the case of Little, Brown and Company, it was noted in a letter of May 18th, 1948, and reinforced in a subsequent one a few weeks later on June 9th, no one at the publishing house was able to read Italian and a request was made that a brief synopsis of the two books be sent to them so that they had some idea of what the works were about before they settled on a possible reader for them. On June 22nd, 1948, Charles B. Blanchard of Little, Brown & Company writes Greenburger informing the literary agent that he received a report on *Il compagno* rather than on the agreed *Paesi tuoi* and *Feria d'agosto*. Nevertheless, choosing not to go to the expense of having the two latter works read, Blanchard returned them noting that the chances were very slight that they would be published. Moreover, Blanchard stresses his point about the review process concerning foreign language books when he adds: "I believe you will understand, and do let us, if possible, in the future have a brief synopsis of each book you submit which is in a foreign language." It should also be noted that Rutgers University Press' decision not to examine *Feria d'agosto* was based on the firm's policy not to consider manuscripts in languages other than English.

From April 1949 to April of the following year, there are a few letters that relate to the promotion of, and interest in, *Prima che il gallo canti* and *La bella estate*. On September 20th, 1949, Donald B. Elder of Doubleday and Company writes Greenburger about the decision not to publish *Prima che il gallo canti*: "Sorry to be returning PRIMO CHE IL GALLO CANTO [sic] by Cesare Pavese. We had an immediate reading which indicates that although the author certainly has something on the ball, we don't feel that we can take him on. I think that ROAD TO THE CITY[30] is about all we can do with novelettes." And in a letter of April 10th, 1950, Arthur Ormont, Associate Editor at Farrar, Straus and Company, informs Greenburger of the refusal of *La bella estate*. While Ormont speaks to Pavese's talents and originality, the primary concern is one of translatability:

> We have reached a decision on Cesare Pavese's LA BELLA ESTATE, which, after extended consideration, does not seem for us. I am afraid that the trouble again, despite Pavese's great talents and originality, is untranslatability. This does not mean, of course, that we would not be much interested in his future work, and I do hope you will bear us in mind for it.

A large portion of the correspondence, dating from August 1950 through the end of November of the same year, pertains to the marketing and publication rights of Pavese's latest novel *La luna e i falò*. In a letter dated October 17th, 1950, Greenburger writes London-based literary consultant Charles G. Bode and shares the impressive list of American publishers interested in considering

---

[30] N. Ginzburg's novella *The Road to the City* (*La strada che va in città*) was published by Doubleday and Company in 1949.

Pavese's novel.[31] Greenburger also references the intention of sharing translation costs with British publisher John Lehmann Limited:

> I delayed the answer because my copy of LA LUNA E I FALÒ arrived only a few days ago. Mr. Hubesch[32] is not back from Europe yet and his office knows nothing about it. I did tell them, however, that we have other requests for it and for your information I am giving you the list of those we have promised to show the book, because, evidently, whoever takes it will want to take the Lehman translation:
> 1. Pellegrini & Cudahy
> 2. Farrar, Straus
> 3. Alfred A. Knopf
> 4. Harper & Bros.
> 5. Viking
> 6. Pantheon
> 7. Appleton-Century-Crofts
> 8. Houghton Mifflin
> Of course, there are a great many others who have seen Pavese's previous books and have been interested in him as a writer, although none of the previously published ones seemed suited doe [sic] U.S. publication at the time.

In a letter of October 31st, 1950, Arthur Ormont of Farrar, Straus and Company notifies Greenburger of his publishing firm's serious interest in *La luna e i falò*; however, he raises once again the concern regarding the translatability of Pavese's works. Nevertheless, a cost-share option with the British publishing house of John Lehmann Limited remained a strong incentive to publish Pavese:

> At Roger Straus' suggestion I have today written to John Lehmann requesting information about his projected translation of Cesare Pavese's LA LUNA E I FALÒ which is under serious consideration here. To our minds the problem of Pavese is almost exclusively one of translatability and we are anxious to hear from Lehmann his plans for a translation and his general ideas about introducing Pavese to an English

---

[31] In a letter of September 8th, 1950, C. Bode writes Greenburger informing him that he had learned from Milan of Pavese's suicide and expresses Mr. Lehmann's condolences, along with regrets that "no further books will be available from a very promising author whom he has just taken up." Bode concludes his letter by stating that Mr. Lehmann "will, however, go ahead with the production of *La luna e i falò*."

[32] B. W. Hubesch was a senior editor at Viking Press.

speaking public. Of course the fact that costs can now be shared encourages us considerably.[33]

On November 10th, 1950, Greenburger updates Giulio Einaudi on the status of Pavese's books and speaks to the advantages of going with Farrar, Straus and Company:

> Pellegrini declined the book. The other requests after Straus are Knopf, Hubesch, MacMillan. In view of the fact that British rights are gone, and the nature of the philosophy of the book – I doubt that we will do any better than this. Straus also has a continuing interest in the Italian books, having done well with Levi and their other Italian writers.[34] After he launches Pavese he assured me that he would publish some of the old books if LA LUNA is successful. He had liked some of the previous books but did not think them strong enough at the time to launch an author with.

On November 22nd, 1950, Greenburger sends a signed contract for the U.S. publication of *La luna e i falò* to John Meyer of Farrar, Straus and Company.[35]

In revisiting Pavese's initial steps with the American publishing world, I have sought to shed light on the publishing obstacles and challenges that may have impacted the circulation of his works in the English-speaking world. A fundamental question in this process has been the quality of Pavese's translations in English that have been defined as "critically wrong," "clumsy," "unreliable," and "stilted English prose" by a variety of critics and translators, including Donald Heiney, William Arrowsmith, Leslie Fiedler, and R. W. Flint. Along with the seeming shortage of competent translators at the time Pavese's works were first being circulated, the Piedmontese writer's elliptical and allusive style, as noted by Paolo Milano, made the task of translation a daunting one. Both the archives of the Alfred A. Knopf Publishing Company and of the literary agent Sanford J. Greenburger offer key insights into the process of introducing Pavese to an American readership, his marketability, and the

---

[33] See note 18.

[34] Farrar, Straus, and Company had published C. Levi's *Christ Stopped at Eboli* in 1947 and would continue to show an affection for the Italian writer's works.

[35] Farrar, Straus & Young (as the firm was now called) published *La luna e i falò* (*The Moon and the Bonfires*) in 1953, translated by M. Cecconi. By the time of the publication, Giulio Einaudi Editore had empowered the Agenzia Letteraria Internazionale to act as its agents for the Pavese Estate (See letter by P. McLauglin to Greenburger, dated Novemmber 3rd, 1953, in the Greenburger Collection).

translatability of his works. Furthermore, this archival material highlights Calvino's criticism that the American publishers' biggest economy is made on the translation. In the introduction to his recent translation of *La luna e i falò*, Tim Parks writes that his rendering of the novel has the "the advantage of a forty-year fascination with Pavese's work" (Pavese 2021, xxv). Parks' long experience with Pavese's texts is based on the premise that "much can be learnt about a work of literature by considering the problems involved in its translation" (Parks 1998, vii). His introduction is a reminder of the type of challenges that the reader, not to mention a potential foreign publisher, faces when encountering Pavese's works: "Pavese doesn't come to us for praise, or even approval, and it's precisely as he tries to put a damper on our enthusiasm, that we feel more powerfully attracted to him" (Pavese 2021, xiv).

Archives

Alfred A. Knopf, Inc. Records (Manuscript Collection MS-00062). Harry Ransom Center, The University of Texas at Austin. Folders 29.6, 31.6, 47.1, 67.5, 295.4, 327.10

Giulio Einaudi Editore. State Archive of Turin (Italy). Cesare Pavese Folder, Mario Einaudi Folder and Sanford J. Greenburger Folder

Giulio Einaudi Editore, Archivio di Stato di Torino. Turin, Italy. Folders 74 and 132.1

Sanford J. Greenburger Literary Agency Records, Ax 801, Special Collections & University Archives, University of Oregon Libraries, Eugene, Oregon. Box 13

Bibliography

Calvino, I. (2013). *Letters: 1941-1985*, translated by M. McLaughlin, edited by M. Wood. Princeton-Oxford: Princeton University Press

Cambon, G. (1977). "Truth as Fiction: Pavese's Diary", *Michigan State Quarterly Review*, 16(1), pp. 1-10

Casson, L. (1965). "Night Thoughts from Olympus", *Saturday Review*, June 5, p. 25

Della Terza, D. (2001). D*a Vienna a Baltimora. La diaspora degli intellettuali europei negli Stati Uniti d'America*. Roma: Editori Riuniti

Flint, R. W. (1968). "Translating Cesare Pavese", *Delos*, 1, pp. 152-164

Healey, R. (1998). *Twentieth-Century Literature in Translation: An Annotated Bibliography 1929-1997*. Toronto: University of Toronto Press

Heiney, D. (1968). *Three Italian Novelists: Moravia, Pavese, Vittorini*. Ann Arbor: The University of Michigan Press

Hyman, S. E. (1968). "Sad Encounters", *The New Yorker*, 44(27), August 24th, p. 114

Lihua, Y. and MacShane, F. (eds). (1986). *The Journal of Literary Translation. Special Issue: The Italian Book in America: Il libro italiano in America*. New York: Columbia University, Translation Center

Milano, P. (1951). "A Literary Letter about Italy", *New York Times Book Review*, 21, January, p. 28

Paige, D. D. "Italian Letter", *Intro*, Vol. II, I (1952), pp. 21-25

Pavese, C. (1961). *This Business of Living, Diary: 1935-1950*, translated by A. E. Murch. London: Owen

——— (2021). *The Moon and the Bonfires*, translated by T. Parks. London: Penguin Books

Smith, L. G. (2010). *Pavese in America: A New Beginning*, in Cerrato, T. and Brandone, G. (eds.). *Incontro con Cesare Pavese: un giorno di simpatia totale*. Atti del convegno di studi Convitto Nazionale Umberto I Liceo Classico D'Azeglio, Torino, 23-24 ottobre 2008, Quaderno n. 3, Liceo Classico D'Azeglio Torino, pp. 165-172

Venuti, L. (1982). "The Art of Literary Translation: An Interview with Lawrence Venuti", *Denver Quarterly*, 17, Summer, pp. 16-26

Further Reading

Fiedler, L. (1954). "Introducing Cesare Pavese", *Kenyon Review*, 16(4), pp. 536-553

Mangoni, L. (1999). *Pensare i libri. La casa editrice Einaudi dagli anni Trenta agli anni Sessanta*. Turin: Bollati Boringhieri

Parks, T. (1998). *Translating Style. The English Modernists and Their Italian Translations*. London-Washington: Cassell

Pavese, C. (1954). *The Moon and the Bonfires*, translated by L. Sinclair. New York: Signet Book

——— (1966). *Lettere 1945-1950*, edited by I. Calvino. Turin: Einaudi

Smith, L. G. (2008). *Cesare Pavese and America*. Amherst: University of Massachusetts Press

Chapter 6

Recognizing Oneself in a Distorted Mirror: The Irresolvable Transnational Distance and Proximity Between Pavese and Pasolini[1]

Francesco Chianese

Cardiff University (UK) / California State University Long Beach

Abstract

The literary careers of Cesare Pavese and Pier Paolo Pasolini overlapped for about eight years, from 1942 to 1950, but were based in separate contexts that the war did not bring any closer. The distance between them grew subsequently within criticism, as mostly scholars worked separately on them despite their shared interests, like their fascination for the Greek myth and the United States. Nonetheless, a comparison between Pavese and Pasolini relying upon the identification of common topics does not always produce similarities, but it is a productive approach for deepening the understanding of their radical difference. Building upon a series of points of contact between Pavese and Pasolini – their contradictory definition of otherness, their preference for the myth, their attraction to the United States and ancient Greece, their passion for psychoanalysis and anthropology – this essay aims to connect Pavese and Pasolini through their distance, pointing out how the elements that they show as common increase their difference in significant ways.

---

[1] This contribution was revised and published as part of the research project *TransIT–Many Diasporas from One Transnational Italy.* This project has received funding from the European Union's Horizon 2020 research and innovation programme under the Marie Skłodowska-Curie grant agreement No. 892584. The REA is not responsible for any use that may be made of the information it contains.

Keywords: Pavese; Pasolini; Transnationalism; Otherness; Lacanian theory; Literary Engagement

* * *

1. Introduction: Comparing Through Difference

In a period when the transnationalization of Italian studies is firmly on the agenda, it is surprising that two contemporary writers who repeatedly stressed the need to analyze Italian 0 beyond its national boundaries, Cesare Pavese and Pier Paolo Pasolini, have rarely been read alongside each other. Here I intend the term "transnationalization" in the wider meaning of a process seeing the expansion of Italian culture in the direction of global and cross-cultural trajectories (Bond 2014; Burdett and Polezzi 2020). This is an analytical framework through which Pavese and Pasolini have not been discussed often, either together or individually (Chianese 2015), although they demonstrated a deep level of concern for the ways Italy was adapting to the global transformations occurring in the aftermath of the Second World War. In their *oeuvre*, they attempted to problematize the process that was radically changing the Italian identity, acknowledging two subsequent moments in the evolution of the country into one of the biggest industrial forces and international markets.

The attention devoted to the evolution of Italian culture within the global context was probably the most striking feature that Pavese and Pasolini shared in their profile as intellectuals and authors. This was the starting point for the only monograph reading the two writers alongside one other: *Dittico: Pavese, Pasolini*, published by Ettore Perrella in 1979. This is also the starting point for my comparative reading of the two authors. My investigation of their works will follow a different trajectory, while insisting on conceiving Pavese and Pasolini as part of a diptych – "dittico" – that does not find a conciliation. It rather identifies an irresolvable dualism between two radically different personalities that encounter each other in the recognition of similar issues, to which they suggest different, often opposite approaches (Perrella 1979, 9). In fact, two is the number of the encounter, a topic that they both privileged in their works, as well as of contradiction: two elements that contrast each other. Perrella's metaphor that sees Pavese and Pasolini as two altar panels with no central image between them appears appropriate, because the story of their encounter is yet to be written (Perrella 1979, 9). This image explicitly recalls Pasolini's "anti-Hegelianism," in which a thesis and an antithesis do not conciliate in a synthesis, but establish two truths affirming each other through their opposition. An accurate comparison between Pavese and Pasolini has not been written because it cannot be addressed by walking regular critical patterns. On those premises, Carla Benedetti compared Pasolini and Italo Calvino, an author who was a close friend of both Pavese and Pasolini, by identifying their different approach to postmodernism (Benedetti 1998). Most scholars insisted on the similarities between the two writers rather than their differences (see Palazzo 1998; Focchi 1979; Marchesini 2017). By contrast, Marco Antonio Bazzocchi opposed Pasolini to Pavese through their dissimilar conceptions of myth, after recognizing them as the only two contemporary Italian writers who considered it with solid cognitive intentions (Bazzocchi 2011). Despite not sharing common arguments, both Perrella and Bazzocchi pointed out the necessity of a peculiar, paradoxical method to investigate Pavese and Pasolini within the same critical framework. I agree with them in observing that the same movement bringing them next to each other through the identification of a series of common topics, which underscores their original contribution to Italian culture, is balanced by an opposite movement highlighting their distance when we examine the ways they explored those topics. Close but distant, they appear to look at one other through a distorting mirror, each contemplating his altered reflection through the other. This image captures the similar, oscillatory, often contradictory approach to reality that both authors featured in their works, which particularly stands out from the ways they described their relationship with otherness in terms of simultaneous fascination and trauma. Pasolini identified contradiction as one of his keywords, which has been frequently used in the context of the studies on his *oeuvre*. Sergio Givoni has seen in Pavese's way to introduce myth a sign of contradiction, especially in his *Dialoghi con Leucò* (Givone 1999, VI). In particular, both Pavese and Pasolini seem to have based their experience with the rural world and the major phase of their production on the contradiction between amazement and shock. Looking at the countryside from the viewpoint of the urbanized individual, they recognized in it the world of origins, towards which they romanticized the return.

Pavese was fourteen years older than Pasolini. Chronologically, their careers as writers overlapped for about eight years, from 1942 to 1950, but were based in separate contexts that the experience of war did not help to bring any closer. When Pasolini's debut collection *Poesie a Casarsa* came out in 1942, he was a student at the University of Bologna and was engaged in literary magazines between Emilia and Friuli; Pavese was an established poet, novelist, and translator based in Turin, about to become a pillar of the Italian publisher Einaudi. After the war they lived in the same city, Rome, but at different moments: Pavese between 1945 and 1946, returning for a shorter period from late December 1949 to early January 1950. Pasolini moved to Rome a few weeks later, in late January 1950, and resided there for the following 25 years of his life until his death. Their experience in Rome was different and identified the capital city as a different place, as we witness when comparing Pavese's *Il compagno* (1947) with Pasolini's *Ragazzi di vita* (1955) and *Una vita violenta* (1959). Reading in parallel their divergent descriptions of Rome allows us not only to highlight the multiplicity of approaches to describing the same city within the same cultural context. It also captures the wide diversity of the Italian capital, its inner complexity and polymorphic nature, and points to the significant changes that the city underwent in the few years between Pavese's journey and Pasolini's relocation. Their view of Rome showcased Italy's deep transformations already evident in the aftermath of the war to the beginning of the 1950s.

The distance between Pavese and Pasolini grew within criticism. Pasolini's negative judgement of Pavese's work, on which he dwelt at length and not in the nicest way, may have contributed to the reciprocal diffidence between scholars working on each of them (Gutiérrez 1972). Nonetheless, as stated by Massimo Fusillo, literature features unexpected connections that are independent from writers' intentions (Fusillo 2007). Among the scholars working on Pasolini, Fabio Vighi emphasized the value of "traumatic encounters" in Pasolini's formation, as well as his ability to find similarities with surprising authors, such as filmmaker Werner Fassbinder (Vighi 2006; Vighi and Nouss 2010). Similarly, Pasolini's representation of *Medea* on screen has been compared with the transposition of the Greek myth from another German author, Christa Wolf's novel *Medea* (1996). Approaching Greek myth, Pavese and Pasolini encountered a peculiar, common ground that strengthened their dialogue despite Pasolini's severe opinion of Pavese and his hasty way of sustaining it. Their fascination for the United States further contributed to their conversation.

Ultimately, a comparison between Pavese and Pasolini stresses that comparing two writers through the identification of common topics and concerns does not always produce similarities. Sometimes it deepens the understanding of their radical difference. Therefore, starting from a series of points of contact between them – their contradictory definition of otherness, their preference for the myth, their attraction to the United States and ancient Greece, their passion for disciplines such as psychoanalysis and anthropology – I will set the ground on which their dialogue was built through their distance, pointing out how the elements that they show as common in fact increase their difference.

2. From Dialogue to Contradiction:
The Self and the Other Between Fascination and Trauma, the City and the Country, the Rational and the Irrational

Pavese's internment in Brancaleone was a foundational experience in his formation as a novelist (Chianese 2020). We can witness Pavese's own unsettling experience in the ancestral and peasant world in Stefano's account in *Il carcere*, which was not published until 1948 but was mostly written in 1939, before Pavese's first novel *Paesi tuoi* was published in 1941 (it was written in 1939, too). Those two works resonate with each other: Pavese delves into his autobiography and investigates his liminal position between the stability of the urban context and the call from an irrational feeling originating outside the city borders. The boundary between those aspects is thin in Turin, the city where Pavese spent most of his life, as everybody who has some familiarity with the city knows: the river Po separates the city center from the hill. This boundary is thin within the human mind as well. In Pavese's fiction, Turin's urban structure becomes a metaphor for the conflict between the rational and the irrational, which has been highlighted as one of his most recurrent topics. On this opposition is based his traumatic representation of the encounter with the other, which inspired his interest in ethnography and anthropology.

Unexpected encounters abound in literature. Meeting the unforeseen often emerges as a traumatic event in a conservative culture such as the Italian culture. The intolerance for Italy's stale character was at the basis of a common dissatisfaction that Pavese shared with Pasolini, which paved the way for their unlikely connection. Both writers started their careers with poetry, on which neither of them based their major phase. Pavese's fiction and Pasolini's cinema originated from a traumatic event that shook their stability, around which they reconfigured their identity as authors and individuals. Pavese's traumatic event can easily be identified in his imprisonment by Fascist police and subsequent internal exile to the South. When he returned to Turin, it was followed by the discovery that the woman he loved, who also was responsible for his arrest, was not a trustworthy Penelope: in his absence, she had married another man. Related to a sexual scandal resulting in permanent ostracism from his romanticized Friuli, Pasolini's shock further compromised the acceptance of his already troubled homosexuality. Their experience of *catabasis* put them in touch with a different variety of humanity, in this finding some similarities with the experience of undeserved exile that inspired Dante's *Divine Comedy*. Despite the feeling of alienation at times recognized in the Calabrian landscape, of which we find witness in *Il mestiere di vivere*, Pavese found a new motivation through contact with the Southern peasant. In the inhabitants of Brancaleone, he recognized similarities with the people from Langhe, where he spent his childhood. Pasolini found similarities with Friulian youth in the innocence and spontaneity of the subproletariat inhabiting Roman suburbs. My argument is based on the assumption that for both Pavese and Pasolini, the traumatic encounter carried the opposite, positive outcome, introducing them to new contexts of experience. All in all, Pasolini demonstrated a wider openness to the unexpected than Pavese, which we can distinguish in many contexts. In the *Manifesto per un nuovo teatro*, for example, Pasolini maintained that the only way to approach his new theatre was to ignore any pre-existing idea of theatre (Pasolini 1998). His attitude to exploring new contexts was witnessed in his recurrent shifts from one field to another, resulting in an incessant creative restlessness and the decision to start a career as a filmmaker at the age of 38, evidencing an unexhausted desire to face new challenges. Conversely, Pavese's hostility to the unexpected was well-known among his friends and colleagues.[2] However, in the antithetical inclination towards the rational and the irrational resides for both Pavese and Pasolini the deepest nature of otherness, to which they were equally attracted and repulsed, but which they have equally investigated in their writing. A substantial contradiction in Pavese appears in this contrast between his intolerance for the narrowness of Italian culture, which urged him towards the unknown American culture, and the uneasiness shown in his encounters with otherness. I believe Pasolini and Pavese truly find each other in their contradictory attitude, which in relation to Pasolini, Franco Fortini defined as a subspecies of *oxymoron*, known in ancient rhetoric as *sineciosis*, by which two opposites statements about the same subject are affirmed (Fortini 1993, 22).

Thematically speaking, a superficial reading of Pavese and Pasolini side by side would reveal more similarities than differences, despite their evidently distinct styles and Pasolini's choice to export his key topics, which he used to define obsessions – "ossessioni" – beyond the page. The rural nostalgia that one identifies in their works is constantly opposed to the urban context in which they lived as adults. From their urban viewpoint, the rural context – in Brancaleone, in the Langhe, in Friuli or in Morocco – is categorized as other and romanticized as an original paradise, from which both authors seem to be excluded. In their *oeuvre*, they both sought figures embodying the primitive spontaneity that they see in people inhabiting the countryside. Similarities between the environment Pavese described in *Il carcere* and *Paesi tuoi* can be recognized in Pasolini's early novels set in Friuli, *Atti impuri* and *Amado mio* (1982), as well as his play *Bestia da stile* (1979), on which he worked from 1966 to his last days, all published posthumously and highly autobiographical. The characters shown in all those texts are conceived as living in a pre-civilized, pre-historicized context; in Pasolini's mature works, this characterization acquires a deeper meaning, contrasting with the concurrent evolution of consumerist society. The differences between the two authors intensify if we observe that Pavese profoundly problematized his view of what we may define as a rural subaltern, by taking inspiration from Gayatri Spivak's reconceptualization of Antonio Gramsci's theories (Spivak 1988). Urban characters such as Pavese's

---

[2] N. Ginzburg wrote about Pavese that the unexpected used to make him feel uncomfortable: "L'imprevisto lo metteva a disagio" (Ginzburg 1963, 199).

alter-egos Stefano and Berto and Pasolini's alter-egos Paolo and Jan crashed against the radical incomprehensibility of a context defined by rites related to blood, sex and death and marked by a different concept of time and life, with which they have no familiarity. Their characterization underscores a detached, at times ethnographic perspective, from which the reader witnesses Berto's shock when faced with Gisella's death in *Paesi tuoi* and his discomfort at discovering the incestuous nature of her brother Talino's attraction for her. An analogous feeling of disconcertment accompanies Stefano's introduction to the sexual relationship between Concia and the men of Brancaleone, which is defined as a spontaneous rite of passage by the inhabitants of the village. In *La luna e i falò*, this unsettlement is shown by the peasant returning from his American experience, like the protagonist of Pavese's early poem *I mari del sud*: here, Pavese's narrative appears to define a circular structure, with the outcast discovering again his hometown as it was the first time. In the same vein, *Bestia da stile* introduces Jan's suicide in the Friulian countryside camouflaged as the Czech village of Semice, while he acknowledges his irresolvable difference from the local boys (Pasolini 2001). In Pasolini's case, the viewpoint of the outcast is also characterized by his sexually non-conforming identity, but *Atti impuri* and *Amado mio* confirm that the nature of the urban detachment prevails. Nonetheless, in essays such as *Limitatezza della storia e immensità del mondo contadino* (1974), Pasolini confirms that the innocence and purity of the rural subaltern, in its radical incomprehensibility to the urban self, is an absolute that for him cannot be questioned or problematized, becoming a myth through its very nature. Pasolini's approach to his subject is made more complex through the multiplicity of his forms of expression, while the indisputable positivity of the rural subaltern becomes a stable pole constantly opposed to everything he considered as negative in Italy, and in the world at large. According to Fusillo, Pasolini's escape from literature into cinema was a quest for a form of expression, in which he discovered a new language that was not corrupted by consumerism, featuring the purity and the innocence he needed to describe his romanticized subject (Fusillo 2007, 14).

In their different approaches, we detect the centripetal tension of Pavese's attitude in pushing the boundaries of literature from the inside, against Pasolini's centrifugal dynamism that breaks those boundaries, escaping literature towards hybrid forms contaminating writing with visual language. Furthermore, Pavese introduced into Italian literature issues and forms that he discovered in his work as a translator, but he never crossed his national boundaries in life. In fact, Perrella defined Pavese's passion for the United States a love afar – an *amor de lonh* – which is already a figure of otherness. Conversely, Pasolini constantly traveled the world he described. Hence, when his search for the rural subaltern in Italy appeared exhausted, he started seeking this figure in Africa and Asia, while investigating the homologous urban type inhabiting the ruins of consumerist Italy in Roman suburbs and later Naples. Despite their difference, the conflict between the rational and the irrational arises around the bipolar opposition on which both writers built their *oeuvre*. They addressed their fascination for the irrational without renouncing their rational approach to culture and reality. Quite the opposite in terms of temper and attitude, the serious and reserved Pavese and the provocative and unconventional Pasolini kept themselves grounded in their approach to life that at times appears excessively cerebral, while describing the primitive nature of their characters. In Pavese, this translated into the solid structure of his novels, which never question the order of reality. Conversely, Pasolini often appeared hostage to the chaos of his radical concept of realism, in which everything finds its place if considered within the wider architecture recognizable in his entire production.

3. Knowing the Other Through Transnationalism and Myth: The Rural Subaltern Between the United States and Ancient Greece, and What This Has to Do With Nietzsche

According to Bazzocchi, Pasolini and Pavese used a specific method to address myth in their work. Bazzocchi also stated that their methods differ radically from each other: for Pasolini, reality gave significance to myth, while conversely, Pavese interpreted reality through myth, cohering with the ways myth has been elaborated in psychoanalysis and anthropology (Bazzocchi 2011). Nonetheless, their different paths were inspired, again, by a dualistic approach, through which we understand their common topics and concerns. Fortini defined Pasolini's antithetical stance by using two words taken from the Greek lexicon – *oxymoron* and *sineciosi* – through which it is possible to affirm two opposite statements about the same object at the same time. Those Greek words recall the ways Pavese and Pasolini looked at Western society, going backwards from its most recent evolution in the contemporary United States to the ancient Greek model, in which they acknowledged a condition that pre-existed capitalism and the civilization and politics producing it. In this context, they identify a subaltern, barbaric figure who escaped fascism by pre-existing it. Even though they followed a diverse path, their elaboration of myth aimed to answer the same question and was directed to the same arrival point: the individuation of an anti-intellectual character who strengthened the meaning of their own intellectual figure by opposing it. The opposition between the two forces underlined the possibility of a devolution towards a more spontaneous condition, able to tackle contemporary social and political transformations.

I believe that focusing on Pavese's and Pasolini's approach to myth is the most profitable way to carry out a comparison between them. Their mythical method is only partially recognizable in their reconfiguration of the ancient Greek tradition, which they addressed specifically only after building into their previous works a sophisticated net of symbols reminiscent of a mythical structure pre-existing reality. Furio Jesi's anthropological reading of Pavese's works is crucial in clarifying his approach to myth and literature. Jesi's use of the verb "clarifying" is essential, because, according to him, Pavese's theory of myth aimed to reduce myth to clarity through literature (Jesi 1964, 115). Deep down, Jesi's assumption seems to associate Pavese's interpretation of the relationships between literature and myth to the modernist approach spearheaded by authors such as T. S. Eliot and James Joyce, with whom he had a certain familiarity. Not by coincidence, Pavese was the author of a critically acclaimed translation of Joyce's *The Portrait of the Artist as a Young Man* (*Dedalus: Ritratto dell'artista da giovane*, 1933). This shows that for Pavese, literature is still conceived as an instrument to restore the order of a world overturned by war. Conversely, Pasolini's approach to myth may rather be defined as postmodern, pointing out the need to reconceptualize myth in accordance with radically different literary models. Jesi's reading of the myth in Pavese resonates with Fusillo's interpretation of myth in Pasolini. Fusillo maintained that Pasolini viewed literature in relation to the 'Oedipal desire' to break codes and cross boundaries, highlighting a tendency towards contamination and hybridity (Fusillo 2007, 12). Their contrasting approaches to myth proceed in part from their distinct historical contexts: Pavese never witnessed the transformations Italy underwent between the 1950s and the 1970s, which inspired Pasolini's cynicism and skepticism regarding the possibility of restoring the old world. Here also lies Pasolini's more radical regret for the loss of the pre-national and pre-industrial peasant world. For Pasolini, the order that Pavese both problematized and romanticized was lost forever. Literature and cinema were considered as escape strategies, allowing the construction of an alternative context, while simultaneously romanticizing the past through a feeling of nostalgia. This nostalgia nonetheless needs to be contextualized, as Pasolini emphasized in his reply to Calvino's criticism (Pasolini 1975). Furthermore, the difference between Pavese and Pasolini also relates to the different evolution of their biographies. Pavese experienced a temporary exile marked by the return to Turin, which he translated into his recurrent topic of the homecoming. By contrast, Pasolini's expulsion from Friuli was experienced as a permanent *damnatio* without the possibility of restoring the old harmony. Hence Pavese never crossed the boundary between reality and what stands beyond it, as Jesi underscored, which is the issue that made him appear to Pasolini as a "correct" intellectual and provoked his disappointment. According to Fusillo, through contamination and pastiche Pasolini aimed to recreate the atemporal language of myth to build a separate dimension from the corrupted present reality (Fusillo 2007, 22). Both authors found in myth an escape from an equally unsatisfying reality, though their differing outcomes brought them, if possible, even further from each other.

Nonetheless, the pair overlap in a sort of Benjaminian double-step, as both authors were guided towards the past of ancient Greece while looking to the future, to the United States and beyond the confines of Western civilization (Perrella 1979, 81-82; Trentin 2013, 1021-1041). Fusillo stressed that Pasolini defined this process as "transnational": his intention was to share through myth and cinema a message that could be universally understood anywhere and in any language. Pavese's oscillation between ancient Greece and the United States was also transnational, because in both, he looked for a rural Italy that was devastated by civil war, isolating a happy community that somehow seems to have paved the way for Pasolini's more radical anti-consumerist message.

According to Lorenzo Mondo, Pavese elaborated his theory on myth when he was hiding on the hill in Monferrato (Mondo 1961, 16). This moment has been considered as a watershed in Pavese's fiction. The Christian-Marxist syncretism identified by Mondo in Pavese's post-war writings seems to anticipate Pasolini's contradictory approach to Catholic religion, which oscillates in his cinema between a more orthodox view shown *Il vangelo secondo Matteo* (1964) and a pagan recontextualization in *Edipo re* (1966). Pasolini probably did not receive this more ambivalent perception of Pavese's thought from the conventional reading established shortly after his death. We do not know, for example, if Pasolini ever read Jesi's essay proving a more complex view of Pavese's approach to literature. It was published while Pasolini was immersed in his work on Greek tragedy, resulting in the films *Edipo Re* and *Medea* and his original adaptations *Teorema* (1968) and *Porcile* (1969), as well as his theater. Many critics pointed out that exploring Pavese's theory of myth broadens the interpretation of his thinking, the philosophic depth of which goes beyond the surface of the traditional image of the writer established over the years. According to Giuseppe Zaccaria, Pavese's symbolism was pursued through the study of Giambattista Vico, whose works later inspired postcolonial studies and Eduard Said's *Orientalism* (1978) (Zaccaria, 2009a and 2009b). Mondo and Zaccaria pointed out the prominent role the rediscovery of Greek culture had on Pavese's meditation on myth, of which *Dialoghi con Leucò* (1947) constituted the major outcome (Givone 1999, V). They also pinpointed a sophisticated symbolism in Pavese's early works, where myth appears under the sign of totality and unicity. This symbolism is deeply rooted in childhood, when it is experienced through a free and unconditioned interaction with nature (Zaccaria 2009b, 39). Furthermore, Pavese specifies that a myth is always symbolic, consequently, it never holds a unique, allegorical meaning aiming to a 'sacred eternity,' in which we perceive a reference to Friedrich Nietzsche's theory of the 'eternal return.' Again, Pavese seems to get inspiration from a common anti-Hegelianism, when he defines myth as an absolute that is life in its simultaneous emptiness and fullness, constituting a foundational moment that in its own nature is impossible to define (Zaccaria 2009b, 39). Hence Pavese and Pasolini place the confines of myth outside of space time, both identifying a metaphysical idealism that for Pavese originated in Plato's thought and in the work of Dante, Shakespeare and Dostoevskij (Pavese 1952, 348). Alongside Dante's mysticism, Zaccaria discusses Pavese's psychoanalytical-anthropological background, the same background inspiring Pasolini's cinematic *Oedipus Rex*.

Mondo identifies in Pavese's view of myth the attraction for the irrational that Nietzsche discovered in Greek tragedy, which once again leads to childhood. Pavese stated that one sees things twice: a first innate and original "vision" as children, upon which all subsequent memories of things are built (Pavese 1952, 250). Hence we cannot see things for the first time, we always see them for the second time; the original condition can only be found again in short epiphanic moments in which we completely connect with mythic elements of nature, to the cancellation of ourselves (Zaccaria 2009b, 42). Eventually, according to Zaccaria, Pavese's symbolic reality presents a synthesis of the particular and the universal, which aims to put together what is experienced as fragmented and dispersed, if not oppositional, in an extreme attempt to rationalize the irrational. On Zaccaria's premise, we distinguish in Pavese's works a series of recurring elements which, like Pasolini's 'obsessions,' adjust the writing to the monotone, recurring, obsessive character of myth (Zaccaria 2009b, 47). Detecting the core of their myth in the rural figures inhabiting Langhe and Friuli, characterized by their visceral, at times pagan, approach to religion shown through traditions and popular celebrations, both authors set their narrative challenge on the possibility of connecting myth to the reality they romanticized. By walking in Mondo's footsteps, it appears that both Pavese's and Pasolini's works were built on the aim of finding a balance between order and disorder, which is deeply rooted in what Nietzsche theorized as the equilibrium between the Apollonian and the Dionysian character of Greek tragedy in *The Birth of Tragedy* (1872). Pavese's and Pasolini's narratives recognized the deepest problem of Western civilization in the attention given to our rational side at the expense of the total removal of any irrational feeling. Hence reading their *oeuvre* in the light of Nietzsche's philosophy brings their comparison to a deeper level, especially considering their recurrent references to tragedy and the tragic. Both authors were readers of Nietzsche: Pavese asked to receive *The Birth of Tragedy* and other works by Nietzsche in Brancaleone; Nietzsche's *On The Future of Our Educational Institutions* (1872) was found in Pasolini's car on the night of his murder. Their Christian-Marxist syncretism underscores an extensive knowledge of *Thus Spoke Zarathustra* (1883-85), from which we perceive recurrent images of the 'death of God' and the 'eternal recurrence of the same' in their works.

Ultimately, Pavese and Pasolini translated myth into the same contexts – the American myth, the Greek myth, and the myth concerning the subaltern from the precapitalist world – but finding a different, original meaning. Both inspired by Nietzsche, they find the epicenter of their reflections on myth in their approach to the Greek classics. Their interest in the classic myth is not to be read as an escape from the present, but rather an elaboration on reality, providing a deeper interpretation of their present. They return to myth to find an archaic knowledge embodied by their primitive figures, which holds a forgotten wisdom, and they need to find it in the context in which myth appears at its purest: ancient Greece. By contrast, their view of the United States was profoundly different. Pavese found the barbaric, young and innocent America portrayed in essays such as "L'influsso degli eventi" in the rural suburbs of Oakland, where Anguilla recognized his Piedmontese fellows in *La luna e i falò* (Pavese 1968). This evidences that Pavese's internationalism overlaps with his provincialism (Perrella 1979, 20). Pasolini, on the other hand, found his romanticized subaltern in the African and Asian locations of his cinema, while in the United States, he sought an intellectual youth to whom he devoted the most intimate message of his *oeuvre* (Pasolini 1999). Furthermore, in *La luna e i falò* Pavese described the possibility of merging Greek and American myth though the return of Anguilla to his rural birthplace, which elaborates on the myth of the return of Ulysses as a classical *topos*, as well as one of the foundational narratives of American culture. It symbolized the complicated balance between attraction and repulsion towards the place of origin, which Pavese translated into the image of the village appearing as a place that acquires meaning only when one leaves it (Pavese 1950). In this way, Pavese returned to the spaces of his childhood through the reinvention of the Greek classics, which he studied in the year of his formation, through his subsequent readings: Nietzsche, existentialism, anthropology, psychology, and psychoanalysis. Here resides the preference for childhood as a dimension that pre-exists our perception of time, in an eternal perspective where we can perceive things in their absolute nature, rather than attempting to name and classify them. According to Pavese, mythopoesis consists of translating symbols and myths into words through a process of loss of innocence, which turns the wonder in suffering into the painful truth from which everything originates. Here Pavese joins Pasolini in discovering the truth behind nature when something forbidden brings nature back to its wildest state, revealing the authentic pain of existence (Pavese 1952, 284). By stating that myth is, at the same time, something necessary and impossible, Pavese again paves the way for Pasolini's contradictory view of myth, which urges both to distinguish the irrational from the rational, regardless of their difference in approach, as underscored by Bazzocchi. At the same time, in their consciousness of the impossibility of reconciling the irrational and the rational lies their need to face the other, despite their awareness of the impossibility of knowing him or her, and their approach to the other as fascination and trauma.

4. Encounter and Otherness in Lacanian Theory

Jesi's concept of infantile mythopoesis – *mitopoeia infantile* – through which Pavese identified the ability to translate the images pertaining to our perception of reality into a form that is recognizable to other people through symbols that we share with them, resonates with the process that Jacques Lacan defined as the passage from the Imaginary to the Symbolic (Jesi 1964, 115). In Lacanian terms, Pavese and Pasolini proceeded from the pure innocent marvel of the Imaginary at the encounter with otherness to the trauma of the Real. My final argument concerns how comparing Pavese and Pasolini through Lacanian theory, following in Perrella's footsteps, allows us to discover more intimate connections between them. Applying psychoanalysis as a tool to investigate two authors showing a vivid interest in this discipline and constantly engaging their subjectivity in their works also strengthens the comparative potential of this methodology. Furthermore, Lacanian psychoanalysis has devoted special attention to the dynamics of the encounter. It has long focused on the traumatic aspects of our interaction with the other. In Lacanian psychoanalysis, the encounter as a tension generated towards otherness, which is unexpected due to its specific nature, finds common ground with ethnology, which was a passion shared by both authors. While Pasolini's work has been investigated through Lacanian theory many times, Perrella's study remains the only attempt to read Pavese in this context, despite established essays investigating his *oeuvre* in a psychoanalytical light (Fernandez 1967; Isotti-Rosowsky 1989; David 1976).

In Pavese's description of myth as something necessary and impossible, we find the core of Oedipus's dilemma, which both Pavese and Pasolini adopted in their adaptation of Sophocles' play and which both introjected through their troubled relationships with their father (Pavese 1947). According to Lacanian theory, our father is 'the big Other' and through our first encounter with him we enter the social world. Our father's otherness introduces us to the need to acquire a symbolic structure on the base of which we can communicate ourselves to the other: it is our first approach to language (Lacan 2002). Similarly, we need to find a common symbolic system to understand the otherness of the village: here lies the abundance of symbols in Pavese's *Paesi tuoi*, where the "collina" (hill) becomes a "mammella" (udder) and Gisella's death is described through image of the slaughter of a rabbit. According to Carlo De Matteis, who reads Pavese through the intersection between psychoanalysis and ethnography, the blood mixing with mud relocates the tragedy within the natural cycle of life and death (De Matteis 1975). An analogous rite announces Jan's suicide in *Bestia da stile*, achieving the self-destructive desire that Pasolini expressed nearly twenty years earlier in the incipit of *Atti impuri*'s, which was written between 1946 and 1949 (Pasolini 1982, 5). Berto's furious reaction after Gisella's death and Jan's elegiac farewell highlight diverse reactions to the entity that Lacan defined as the Real. Berto witnesses the radical strangeness of nature to the urban character and emphasizes its defamiliarizing aspects. He is horrified by the mix of the blood with the mud (Pavese 1941, 79). Jan's decision to kill himself emphasizes a different feeling of not belonging but an equal desire to escape that is found in Pavese's character. In both cases, the Real is presented as a traumatic event that awakens the conscience from the delusions that fed the urban character. As stated, Pavese and Pasolini started their major phase after a traumatic event concerning their encounter with the other. Perrella underlined that in *Il carcere*, Pavese mythicized the village through a series of symbols that exposed his radical otherness to them, making the place itself a function of the other, which as such, defined the self by the other's alterity (Perrella 1979, 61). Hence the path to the other is by definition impossible, because it implies an overlap between the other and the self: in that case, the other would not be other anymore. Consequently, Perrella maintains that the self and the other can only be reunited in the future, which identifies a paradox, on which the feeling of unsettlement and suffering of Pavese's characters is based. In *La casa in collina*, this overlapping between the other and the self appears possible only when the protagonist finds himself in front of the corpses of the soldiers fighting the civil war in the hills. Pavese described the similarities between the dead and the living soldiers, pointing out a common sense of belonging to humanity beyond the national confines, in which we identify a transnational feeling of identity (Pavese 1949b). The otherness that the protagonist recognizes in the dead enemy's face shows the same sign of suffering he sees in himself. Not by coincidence, *La casa in collina* was published together with *Il carcere*, written much earlier, under the title *Prima che il gallo canti* (1949), which again suggests Pavese's conversion to a Marxist-Christian syncretism. On the other hand, the impotence when faced with the body of the dead that looks like us recalls the frustration that separates us from the other in *Il carcere*. The otherness of the other is confirmed by the death that makes the partisan and Gisella different from us again, undermining the possibility of having an actual exchange with them, which also proves that we are alive in front of them. On the common frustration in the face of the impossible are built Pavese's and Pasolini's narratives: both authors attempt to escape the impossible, when they conceptualize the encounter with the other in its possibility, keeping their characters safe from the actual, Real encounter. But it is a delusional process.

Another description of the Real otherness is found in Pavese's account of the relationships between his alter-egos and his female characters, which highlights a desire to preserve the mystery of otherness instead of discovering that feelings may not be reciprocated. We recognize this unsettlement in the weak efforts taken by Stefano to approach Concia in *Il carcere*, resulting in his escape from her wild femininity, and by Berto to seduce Gisella in *Paesi tuoi*. This is confirmed by a recurrent attention to women's naked feet, the parts of the body that literally keep their bodies at a distance. In Pasolini, a similar tension between attraction and rejection is found in Paolo's homosexual relationship with T. The trauma of the encounter is announced by *Atti impuri*'s incipit, announcing an excruciating week (Pasolini 1982, 5). Like *Paesi tuoi* and *Il carcere*, *Atti impuri* denotes a great interest in the description of nature, alongside an attention to the traumatic historical events recollected in *La casa in collina*. Again, Pavese encounters Pasolini on the ground of contradiction: both their works are devoted to the encounter and, at the same time to its denial. Equally contradictory is Stefano's perception of his reclusion in Calabria, constantly admitting and denying his suffering as a person confined in a context so strange to him. For example, in the scene describing Stefano sitting on Brancaleone beach, the positive feelings about the environment that surrounds him are interrupted by the bewilderment for the rise of the sun, in which we witness a crucial case of the irruption of the Real (Pavese 1949a, 6).

According to Perrella, in Pavese, the Real identifies that which always comes back to the same place (Perrella 1979, 52). More generally, for Lacan, the Real identifies everything, excluding the order of the Imaginary, which coincides with the view of the world that an individual builds for himself. As such, the Real is placed beyond the boundaries of the Symbolic, which is the order that structures reality through the usage of a common language, being based on a series of signs shared by a community that certifies our feeling of belonging to it, and which we appropriate during our childhood. This constitutes another reason why Pavese's symbolism is rooted in images of childhood that he shares with his alter-egos. Without going too deeply into the Real, we can consider as a part of the Real everything one individual excludes and refuses to accept from the perception of reality, which relates directly to the concept of Freudian removal, coming back unconsciously. This process of removal of the Real is not part of the Symbolic but makes the Symbolic possible through the exclusion of the Real. In both Pavese and Pasolini, we find the core of the Real in the perception of the radical otherness of the other, excluding any possibility of authentic contact with it. This radical otherness lies in the acknowledgment that we cannot really know the other. In other words, the Real coincides with the gap between the other and the self, this unfulfillable desire perceived in the distance dividing the two entities. We can only embrace the other as other through the acquisition of this gap and this distance, in the love for our difference and for the unexpected nature of the encounter with otherness. While in his writing and life, Pasolini embraced the otherness of the encounter

– with the consequence that we well know – Pavese communicated his inability to coexist with it. Rather than hypothesizing on the authors' psychological profiles, I would detect this reading of the Real in their shift from one form to another, through which they explored the means that appeared more appropriate to the nature of their encounter with the Real. A world ordered into prose is the world that described Pavese's disappointment with his return to Turin, implying the acknowledgment of the trauma of the Real as an assumption: it was the writing form of confinement, which becomes the way he narrates his existential confinement in Turin. By contrast, for Pasolini, the encounter with the trauma that marked the loss of his paradise translated into the need to explore cinema as a new language to portray the multiplicity of his Real.

Consequently, in Pavese and Pasolini, dualism is, quoting Nietzsche, a repetition of the "eternal recurrence of the same" encounter with the other. The path described by Pasolini from *Atti impuri* to *Bestia da stile* finds a homologue to the one taken by Pavese from *I mari del sud* and *La luna e i falò* – identifying their approach to the Real and its consequences – but describes a different narrative: while Pavese repeats his theme of the homecoming, though an unsettling return, Pasolini's narrative constantly acknowledges his fall from heaven. However, we see a common 'death drive' – *todestreibe* – inspiring their characters, which leads Jan to his suicide in literature that recomposes the natural cycle (Pasolini 2001, 830), and according to a recurrent hypothesis, may have pushed Pavese to take his own life.

5. A Conclusion That Does Not Conclude, or Two Unconcealable Ways of Being Transnationally and Politically Engaged

On a deeper level, my analysis of Pavese's and Pasolini's experiences of the Lacanian Real also investigates the difficulties of the politically engaged writer in Italy during the 1930s and 1940s. It identifies, behind the search for a balance between the attraction to the precapitalist irrational and the influence of the rationality pursued by Western capitalism, a more pressing desire to escape from the radical manifestation of irrationality represented by fascism, which from the 1950s Pasolini recognized in a new form in consumerist propaganda. On those premises, both Pavese and Pasolini highlighted their difficulties in embodying the figure of the politically engaged intellectual – "l'intellettuale impegnato" – which is recurrent in Italian tradition and in whom they detected exhaustion and the need for reconfiguration. Despite his committed antifascism, in his works, Pavese emphasized an inability to follow partisan writers such as Beppe Fenoglio. His inability to distinguish the corpses of the partisan soldiers from the others, pointed to a unique condition of humanity regardless of uniforms and nationalities. Conversely, Pasolini belonged to a different generation of antifascism and had to reinvent his role as a politically engaged post-war intellectual. To follow the evolution of his figure, we also need to take into account the murder of Pasolini's brother Guido in the civil war and Pasolini's expulsion from the Italian Communist Party (Belpoliti 2001). Despite their different outcomes, once again, both Pavese and Pasolini answered the same question – contributing to the quest for a new type of politically committed writer, able to restore the balance between the irrational and the rational that was compromised by Fascist propaganda. Considered in the complexity of their spontaneous compulsion towards otherness, Pavese and Pasolini identified a figure of the intellectual featuring a transnational attitude which was quite rare in postwar Italy and contributed to their international acclaim and recognition. This evidenced again the need to carry out a deeper investigation of their *oeuvre* in a comparative framework, to let them dialogue through their differences and advance our knowledge of postwar Italian literature and culture in its transnational significance.

Bibliography

Fortini, F. (1993). *Attraverso Pasolini*. Torino: Einaudi

Fusillo, M. (2007). *La Grecia secondo Pasolini: Mito e cinema*. Roma: Carocci

Ginzburg, N. (1963). *Lessico familiare*. Torino: Einaudi

Givone, S. (1999). *Introduzione*, in Pavese, C. *Dialoghi con Leucò*. Torino: Einaudi, pp. V-XV

Jesi, F. (1964). "Il mito e la scienza del mito", *Sigma*, 3-4, pp. 95-120

Mondo, L. (1961). *Cesare Pavese*. Milano: Mursia

Pasolini, P. P. (1982). *Amado mio, preceduto da Atti impuri*. Milano: Garzanti

——— (2001). *Bestia da stile*, in Pasolini, P. P. *Teatro*. Milano: Mondadori, pp. 995-1115

Pavese, C. (1941). *Paesi tuoi*. Torino: Einaudi

——— (1949a). *Il carcere*, in Pavese, C. *Prima che il gallo canti*. Torino: Einaudi

——— (1952). *Il mestiere di vivere: diario 1935-1950*. Torino: Einaudi

Perrella, E. (1979). *Dittico: Pavese, Pasolini*. Milano: SugarCo

Trentin, F. (2013). "'Organizing Pessimism:' Enigmatic Correlations between Walter Benjamin and Pier Paolo Pasolini", *The Modern Language Review*, 108(4), pp. 1021-1041

Zaccaria, G. (2009b). *Tecnica narrativa e teoria del mito*, in Zaccaria, G. *Cesare Pavese, percorsi della scrittura e del mito*. Vercelli: Mercurio, pp. 35-82

Further Reading

Bazzocchi, M. A. (2011) *Pasolini e il mito* [Online]. Available at https://www.doppiozero.com/materiali/fuori-busta/pasolini-e-il-mito

Belpoliti, M. (2001). *Settanta*. Torino: Einaudi

Benedetti, C. (1998). *Pasolini contro Calvino: Per una letteratura impura.* Torino: Bollati Boringhieri

Bond, E. (2014). "Towards a Trans-national Turn in Italian Studies?", *Italian Studies*, 3, pp. 415-24

Burdett, C. and Polezzi, L. (2020). *Introduction*, in Burdett, C. and Polezzi, L. (eds.) *Transnational Italian Studies.* Liverpool: Liverpool University Press, pp. 1-21

Chianese, F. (2015). "Pasolini tra USA e URSS: L'intellettuale italiano nella guerra fredda", *Between*, 5, 10, December [Online]. Available at: https://ojs.unica.it/index.php/between/article/view/1699

———— (2020). "L'incontro con l'altro come trauma creativo: Da *Il carcere* a *Paesi tuoi*", *Ticontre. Teoria Testo Traduzione*, 13 [Online]. Available at: http://www.ticontre.org/ojs/index.php/t3/article/view/403/302

David, M. (1976). *Letteratura e psicoanalisi.* Milano: Mursia

De Matteis, C. (1975). "Simboli e strutture inconsce in *Paesi tuoi*", *Studi novecenteschi*, 4(11), pp. 205-285

Fernandez, D. (1967). *L'echec de Pavese.* Paris: Grasset

Focchi, M. (1979). "Due eretici: Pavese e Pasolini", *Spirali*, 6, p. 32

Gutiérrez, S. M. (1972). "Pier Paolo Pasolini su Cesare Pavese", intervista di Franco Contini [Online]. *Città Pasolini.* Available at: https://www.cittapasolini.com/post/pier-paolo-pasolini-su-cesare-pavese-intervista-di-franco-fortini-1972

Isotti-Rosowsky, G. (1989). *Pavese lettore di Freud.* Palermo: Sellerio

Lacan, J. (2002). *Family Complexes in the Formation of the Individual*, translated by C. Gallagher. Chippenham: Antony Rowe

Marchesini, M. (2017). "Pasolini e Pavese: Ombre ingombranti", *Il Foglio*, 10 July [online]. Available at: https://www.ilfoglio.it/una-fogliata-di-libri/2017/07/10/news/pasolini-e-pavese-ombre-ingombranti-143464

Palazzo, V. (1998). "Penna Pavese Pasolini: Maledizione e solitudine", *Il Cagliaritano*, January

Pasolini, P. P. (1975). *Limitatezza della storia e immensità del mondo contadino*, in Pasolini, P. P. *Scritti corsari.* Milano: Garzanti, pp. 51-55

———— (1998). "Manifesto per un nuovo teatro", *Nuovi argomenti*, 9, pp. 6-22

———— (1999). *Un Marxista a New York*, in Pasolini, P.P. *Saggi sulla politica e sulla società.* Milano: Mondadori, pp. 1598-1600

Pavese, C. (1947a). *I ciechi*, in Pavese, C. *Dialoghi con Leucò.* Torino: Einaudi, pp. 19-23

———— (1947b). *La strada*, in Pavese, C. *Dialoghi con Leucò.* Torino: Einaudi, pp. 63-68

———— (1949b). *La casa in collina*, in Pavese, C. *Prima che il gallo canti.* Torino: Einaudi

———— (1950). *La luna e i falò.* Torino: Einaudi.

———— (1968). *L'influsso degli eventi*, in Pavese, C. *Saggi letterari.* Torino: Einaudi

Spivak, G. C. (1988). *Can the Subaltern Speak?*, in Nelson, C. and Grossberg, L. (eds.). *Marxism and the Interpretation of Culture.* Urbana: University of Illinois Press, pp. 271-313

Vighi, F. (2006). *Traumatic Encounters in Italian Film: Locating the Cinematic Unconscious.* Bristol: Intellect

Vighi, F. and Nouss, A. (eds.). (2010). *Pasolini, Fassbinder and Europe: Between Utopia and Nihilism.* Newcaste upon Tyne: Cambridge Scholars

Zaccaria, G. (2009a). *Dal mito al silenzio del mito*, in Zaccaria, G. *Cesare Pavese, percorsi della scrittura e del mito.* Vercelli: Mercurio, pp. 137-153

Chapter 7

Pavese Between
European and American Modernisms[1]

Carlo Tirinanzi de Medici
Università degli Studi di Trento, Italy

Abstract

In the last twenty years, the concept of Modernism has grown relevance as a frame to look at Italian literature of the first half of the twentieth century, replacing and/or integrating other, more traditional, categories such as Decadentism. Nonetheless, Cesare Pavese is almost always overlooked by Italian Modernism scholars, who focused mainly on European modernism: with the exceptions of his poetry or *Dialoghi con Leucò*, his works are considered Neorealist. In this contribution, I reassess the relationship between Cesare Pavese and Modernism arguing that many elements of Pavese's writings are derived from American Modernists. Many features of his style are of Modernist descent, as well as the preference for loners, exiled main characters. Other features, like the indifference for psychological representations and the prominence given in his works to events, are quite common in American Modernism. At the bottom of Pavese's works there is the same effort to synthesize, and critically examine, the contrasting features of modernity: while the thematic levels are the same as in European modernists, their rhematic resolution are more similar to those of American modernists.

Keywords: Modernism; Radical perspectivism; representation of the self; Dialectics; Realism; Media

* * *

---

[1] This article was written in Porto San Pancrazio, in Verona, in October 2020. They were exciting moments. I'd like to thank Federica Barboni for her loving hospitality as well as for Alexa.

1.   Modernism and Italy

The goal of this paper is to assess the modernist features of Pavese's writings. While scholars often address the need to put Pavese aside from purely Neorealist writers, this has not led to reconsider him as belonging to a Modernist frame, although Pavese's intellectual links to several modernists. "One of the most isolated voices of Italian culture of the Thirties" (as Pavese wrote on the blurb of the second edition of his collection of poems *Lavorare stanca*) is still looked at as somehow cut off from the cultural and artistic panorama of his time. Given the Anglo-Saxon origins of the category of Modernism, it should come as no surprise that an American scholar, Leslie Fiedler (1954), was probably the first to try and reposition Pavese outside Realism or Neorealism, and to insert him into the Modernist constellation (Fiedler talks of "modernity": in the Fifties, "Modernism" wasn't used) with Mann, Kafka, Yeats, Eliot. Prieto (1993, 65), too, highlights that Juan José Saer mentions Pavese with Kafka, Faulkner, Joyce, and Pound as a "modern" writer. Criticizing the category of Neorealism, Domenichelli (2005, 697) talks of experimentalism for some Neorealist authors, among which Pavese, whose production shows a tension to experimentation (although he thinks more of avant-Garde). Like Domenichelli, Ferraris (2002) links Pavese's narrative choices to the general need for a renewal of narrative techniques. Ferraris talks, more generally, of Pavese's "modernity", and correctly differentiates his prose from that of Mann and Proust, even though many topics and narrative strategies he takes into account (such as the refusal of "naturalism", a tendency to blur narratorial objectivity and its narrative conventions, like the third-person, omniscient narrator) would well be considered typical Modernist features. One of the first, explicit mentions of Modernism in Pavese is made by Ferme in his essay on translations during the Fascist era. Ferme suggests that Pavese wanted to "transfer in Italian culture styles and themes of what [...] is called 'Modernism'" (Ferme 2002, 84). With Ferme and Ferraris, we are at the beginning of the Twenty-First century: it is around that time that Modernism started to be considered as a theoretical frame to understand Italian writers of the first half of the Twentieth century.

In recent years, the concept of Modernism was used to identify literary movements and single authors in different regions and geographies traditionally excluded from this categorization.[2] In Italy, some scholars like Giacomo Debenedetti hinted to such frame (Tortora 2010), but significantly he never mentioned "Modernism". However, this trend has been subverted in the

---

[2] Examples of this process in Spain and in South America are in Shaw 2002 and Rogers 2014. For a theoretical frame of such moves, see Mao and Walkowitz 2009.

last twenty years,[3] and with Cangiano's work (2018), the picture is completed by an assessment of the cultural premises of Italian Modernism and exhaustive research of its philosophical background. Although consensus has not been reached on the chronology of Italian literary Modernism, this concept is now generally accepted among Italianists.[4]

2. Pavese and Italian Modernism Studies

Bearing this chronology in mind, it is easy to understand why it was only in the last ten years or so that scholars have started to talk openly about Pavese's Modernism: before 2000, this category was not used at all among Italianists. Furthermore, Pavese has been usually left apart by Italian scholars of Modernism despite the ties between high Modernists[5] and Pavese. Pavese indeed translated James Joyce's *Portrait of the Artist as a Young Man* and Gertrude Stein's *The Autobiography of Alice B. Toklas* and *Three Lives*: those works influenced his own poetics (Pietralunga 2005; on Joyce, see King 1972), as well as the idea of rhythm he drew from Stein (Billiani 2019). Although suspicious of his prose, Pavese drew from Joyce (and Kafka: Pavese 1990, 229; Ziolkowski 2020, 32-79) in his elaboration of "image-telling", while the structure of *Il carcere* bear strong resemblances to that of Joyce's *Portrait* (Sichera 2000). Furthermore, the strategy of *Lavorare stanca* was drawn by Pavese from Joyce's stream of consciousness (Milani 2009). Nonetheless, Italian scholars of Modernism rarely include Pavese in their works.

In the most recent and comprehensive introduction to Italian Modernism (Tortora 2018), Pavese is mentioned only three times: twice in a chapter which reconstructs the editorial system of the Thirties and once to attribute him to "a new literary season, more realistic and more traditional" (Toracca 2018, 214). Castellana (2010), delineating his idea of "modernist Realism", never mentions Pavese; Baldi explicitly sets him outside Italian Modernism, stating that he followed "different roads" (Baldi 2010, 74). This is partially due to a quite strict timespan for Modernism, which was built upon Debenedetti's hypothesis that considers Italian Modernism as taking place between 1906 and 1929 (the year when Moravia published *Gli indifferenti*: Tortora 2010), although a recognized

---

[3] See at least Somigli and Moroni 2004; Donnarumma 2006; Castellana 2010; Baldi 2010; Luperini and Tortora 2012; Pellini 2016; Bertoni 2018; Tortora 2018a/b.

[4] A critical stance has been taken by Meneghelli 2013.

[5] "High Modernism" is a commonly accepted shorthand which indicates the works, especially those written in the 1920s, by authors who form the core canon of Modernist literature, such as Eliot, Joyce, Pound, Proust, Mann. See Huyssen 1986; Moretti 1987; 2003; Kavaloski 2014.

Modernist such as Gadda (Donnarumma 2006, who extends the timespan to 1950) wrote almost in the same years as Pavese.

Anyway, after the diffusion of the term Modernism among Italian scholars, some have started to link Pavese to this artistic movement. In the still thin scientific literature on Pavese as a Modernist, one should recall two works on *Lavorare stanca* by Kokubo (2017) and Riccobono (2018), and Comparini's reading of *Dialoghi con Leucò* (2017, but his paper on this topic was published in 2013). Kokubo highlights the "ambiguous position" of Pavese, whose works contain typical Modernist features such as collage, multiple points of view, the symbolic power of reality, and the concern towards some aspects of the modern way of life (loneliness, alienation, the dichotomy city-countryside), aside to "Neorealist" elements like colloquial language, a tendency to "narrative objectivity", abundance of popular characters such as peasants or laborers, everyday or popular low setting, and overt social themes.[6] Riccobono takes a more structural stance on Pavese's Modernism (actually, the author employs both "Modernism" and "modernity" to define Pavese's work) as she identifies the "modernity" of Pavese in his poetic fragmentation, with the single lyric acquiring meaning in its syntagmatic distribution inside a complex structure. This is both a typical Modernist way to bind the dispersive and fragmented world into a coherent device (the book, the macro-text), and a way to intensify the sense of each fragment, reaching a maximum of information in a minimum of space (i.e., the epiphany). Comparini focuses on the use of myth in Pavese's *Dialogues with Leucò*. For the critic, the connection between *Leucò* and Modernism is twofold: on one hand, it is Modernist for its "poliphonic realism", due to the radical perspectivism showed by characters ("perspectivism of ontologic consciences of the characters": Comparini 2017, 172) who act "independently" from the author; on the other hand, it is the actualization of myth, which (drawing from Eliot's ideas on "mythical method") becomes a metahistorical sign of a contemporary condition (Comparini 2017, 178).

With a different approach from these scholars, I will try a panoramic overview of Pavese's narratives instead of focusing on single works, albeit with occasional insights in other literary forms used by Pavese, because the narrative encompasses the most part of Pavese's literary production. Observing these works could provide an idea of the pervasiveness of some Modernist elements. in Pavese's works. Due to lack of space, mine will necessarily be a general overview focusing on some conceptual elements of Pavese's poetics. Hopefully, despite the necessary shortcomings of such types of contribution, this will pave

---

[6] As Kokubo acknowledges, it was C. Crocco who cited the Modernist ties of *Lavorare stanca* in her work on Italian Twentieth-century poetry (Crocco 2015, 46).

the road to more specific analysis, offering more textual evidence to the debate. I will observe the similarities between Modernists authors and Pavese through some textual features (characters, representation of psyche and events) and some structural elements (rhythm, montage, and dialogues as ways to give unity to an otherwise fragmented text). Then, I will propose that Pavese's Modernism is linked to the American version of this movement. Finally, I will propose that a deep, common feature among all Modernist authors and Pavese resides in the need to give a synthesis of the contradiction of modernity through the work of art.

3. Textual features: characters, interiority, event

The first similarity between Modernist and Pavese's novels is that Pavese's main characters are always loners, displaced and/or exiled. They are alienated and excluded (De Falco 2020, 16) from what they acknowledge as their own society: for instance, Berto in *Paesi tuoi* and Stefano in *Il carcere* are city dwellers displaced to the countryside by some external force (the State for Stefano, the deuteragonist Talino for Berto), over which they have almost no control. In this situation, they find themselves bewildered by rules and ways of life they do not understand. Similarly, Pablo in *Il compagno* is estranged and alone in his own city: "I thought of the conversations I had had with them all. I hadn't let on to any one of them that I was as lonely as a dog" (Pavese 1959, 6).

Rosetta in *Tra donne sole* is overwhelmed by the hypocritical and subtly violent lifestyle of Turin's high bourgeoisie, while the narrator Clelia does not resolve her sense of strangeness despite her economic and social success. Again, Anguilla in *La luna e i falò* comes back to his village after many years just to ask himself: "Can it be true that at forty, with all I've seen of the world, I still don't know what my village is like?" (Pavese 2021, 8).

In this respect, the conflict between individuals and modern society is well represented in Pavese's writings. The subject is always on the verge of a crisis, both personal and social (involving personal relations and, through the use of Lukácsian typical, relations between classes), both local (the specific events depicted in the novel) and general (the usually negative and disruptive sense and effect of these events on the protagonist's life). Moreover, Pavese seeks to distance his writing from what he considers a feature of old-fashioned novels: the exaggerated traits of the protagonist, who was usually an "extraordinary hero [straordinario eroe]" (Pavese 1990, 114). With this remark, Pavese seems to hint at a typical feature of classical, Eighteenth-century Realism: i.e., the melodramatic imaginary (Brooks 1976). On the contrary, Pavese prefers average men, or even better, in Musil's words, men without qualities. Thus, in such a sketch of history of the novel, the characters move from extraordinary to average, and this average character must be seen with "homeliness" (in English in the original text: the stress is on simplicity) and "indifference" (Pavese 1990, 114.), as we read in the July 28th, 1938 entry of Pavese's diary:

> Modern art, which seems to avoid a plot, simply substitutes for it an artless account of current affairs, a host of infinitesimal details about domestic incidents; instead of characters it has one character only, the average man, who can be any one of us and, indeed, is, under the old clumsy psychological classifications.
>
> The highest peak of this art is attained by a cunning device. Instead of the "average man," presented as an exceptional hero (as in the first period of modem art), the vogue now is to take for our hero an extraordinary character and present him in his normal state, his "averageness." In that way the old conventional classifications are avoided; the writer chooses an abnormal, pathological hero (that being the common conception of "extraordinary"), and follows his activities with a sort of uncritical homeliness (Faulkner? O'Neill? Proust?). (Pavese 2017, 98-99)

In this sense, Pavese focuses on the "individual singularity" of a character: to be interesting, and to be worthy of being narrated, a character does not need any extraordinary quality; their existence, trivial as it may be, is sufficient. This happens because Modernist novels intensify the root of narrations, the interest for the singularity (Mazzoni 2011). This seems to be the sense of another historiographical sketch on the history of (Realist) novel: the tendency to the character's "autobiography".

> The autobiographical origin of related thought in your poetry is on a par with the autobiographical origin of the objective novel, as you have found in Cellini and Defoe. To present real experiences in the form of an account by a third person is a refinement of technique, but surely it must always (? !) begin with reality as known to the writer, and therefore be autobiographical. As happens in your own novels, too. [...] One banal, complicated variation on this theme is the modem technique of having the different characters in the novel all telling their own life story. *(As I Lay Dying* – Faulkner.) (Pavese 2017, 69)

In Pavese's use, "autobiography" is the ability of the character to speak by himself, or, to put it upside down, the ability of the writer to leave room to the character's self. One should note the choice of the word "autobiography" (which is surely a retrospective narration, but it is also one that is addressed to someone: and here I would like to stress the second feature of this term): the expression of character's self is always mediated, a public one. Here is where Pavese seems to detach from the way Modernists usually treat singularities.

Pavese did not have any sympathy for what he called "psychologism", a feature he considered typical of eighteenth-century novel (namely, of Naturalism), since for him the psyche is relevant only as long as it can unveil some otherwise covered aspects of reality (one should think here to the use of psycho-narration by many Modernists). He doesn't want to discover "a new psychological reality", but to multiply "viewpoints that will reveal the riches to be found in the normal conception of realism" (Pavese 2017, 201-202; in such a concept, we can find a strong resonance with Woolf's perspectivism). In this sense, as Ferraris notes, Pavese avoids the psychological description, and anything similar to the direct representation of consciousness as such (Ferraris 2002, 126). He does not want to *express* an interiority, a subjectivity, something he does not value as an interesting poetic object: "Let me be extremely clear: to get a true account of a train of thought [racconto del pensare] I should have to evoke the inner consciousness of someone who meditates on his ways of thinking. And that does not seem a great subject" (Pavese 2017, 54).

At the same time, Pavese seems to be interested in the ways the "autobiography" of his characters acts on their own present situation, i.e., how their interiority (which is based much on their past experiences) deforms their perception of reality, and especially of events. In this sense, he wants to "multiply the points of view": then, the "autobiography" at the base of the novel takes the perspectivist form it has in, say, Faulkner. Indeed, Pavese prefers to tackle the characters' psychology from the outside, and to see how their minds relate with the world. Until *Il diavolo sulle colline*, as Guglielminetti noted, Pavese's style is almost always an "exterior monologue" (Guglielminetti 2001, xxxiv): in *Paesi tuoi*, Berto always seems to speak and not to merely think, even when he reports other people's dialogues or while he tries to interpret what happened on the scene. At the same time, this style "by its very naturalism, it must become a revealing *way of thinking*" (Pavese 2017, 139; italics in the text) and let the reader infer something about Berto, thus inserting a *distance* between the narrator and the character. Also, the third-person narrator of *La bella estate*, although not incarnated in a character (and as such, external to the story), is strictly focalized, thus conveying Ginia's *perception* of the events more than the events themselves. Moreover, in *Tra donne sole*, Clelia tends to be an "objective" narrator of her own story through a "scission of linguistic 'I'" (Isotti-Rosowski 1988, 320).

In this sense, one can understand why Proust's interest for Marcel's thoughts is judged as "garrulous [pettegolo]" (Pavese 2017, 113). This does not mean that characters are deprived of any interiority, but that the author is not interested in its direct representation. What Pavese values is how the narrator, and the characters, relate to reality: in his own words, "the resonance of the events in the deep conscience of the character" (Pavese 1968, 337). Not the accidental movements of thought, "les intermittences du cœur" as Proust called them in his *Recherche*, but the sense of *necessity* given by a specific mind's stance on the world. It is this stance which creates the style of a novel, where 'style' seems to comprise all the ways in which the story is conveyed into the discourse: vocabulary and syntax, but also the ways to present the events, the construction of plot, and so on.

Pavese is less concerned with the character's psychology than High Modernists because of a slightly different idea of what is interesting in a story. For Pavese, as for Aristotle, at the center of a narration (its *mythos*) there are not characters, but events, although in Pavese these are mediated by the narrator's conscience (see on this what has been said before on Clelia): "Narration is [...] made up of [...] a predetermined pattern of events", although "created according to the style that is reality to the narrator" (Pavese 2017, 201). It is for this centrality of events that Pavese states that the narration could not use characters, and that "the greatest Greek story-teller is Herodotus, not Homer" (Pavese 2017, 288). Although Pavese acknowledges that the psyche of the modern man is manifold, and while in his writings the characters' psychology has a major role in the narrative construction, his preference is always to the exterior world, which determinates the development of the story. One should bear in mind the dissatisfaction with the melodramatic plot, with its great events and plot twists. Then, for Pavese, the events could (or should) be the smallest ones, not the great gestures of the romance-melodramatic narrative line. In this sense, Pavese's writing has been associated to that of Ernest Hemingway, an author surely well-known and appreciated by Pavese (Pavese 2017, 286-287; Stein 2007; Pomilio 2019) and whose influence on Pavese is clear in the rarefaction of narration to the essential, particularly in *Paesi tuoi* (Rubeo 2019, 6). More generally, this emersion underscores the minimal events in spite of the bigger nuclei which are regulated by causal links, and such a narrative strategy is typical of Modernism (Mazzoni 2011, 263; see also Eco 1966, 71-72).

These events could be minimal, but the focus should be on what the characters *do* (and not on what they *think* or *feel*). A narrator should always let the readers "discover how such and such a character extricates himself from a given situation" (Pavese 2017, 98). Thus, as stated above, the psychology does not account for a plot *per se*, but as an element which, conditioning the character, influences the plot. It is in this frame that one can read the interest of Pavese for "the true": i.e., what is outside the subject (Isotti-Rosowski 1988,

275-7).[7] This truth is always put under scrutiny by the conscience of characters and narrators, who re-elaborate and determine the sense of what happened. This is clear in the *Dialoghi con Leucò*, where the actors on the scene usually talk about people, thus reframing the narration on another level. Reprising a classical narratological distinction, the events, although present only as reported by the characters, are the focus of the story, while the discourse is orchestrated by the character's interpretation which in turn is organized in a *public discourse* (i.e., they are talking to someone present on the scene).

In this sense, one should note that while working on his novels, Pavese had a special interest in reinforcing and making more evident the isotopies of seeing, talking, and crafting (Grasso 2020): in other words, elements that are *outbound* and, more generally, *exteriorize* the telling.

Also, we can understand his interest in images as part of his event-centered narration. For Pavese, the "image-tale" [immagine-racconto] is a strategy to transfer to the sensible, to the visibile, a "fantastic relationship", i.e., a symbolic one belonging to the subject.[8] This role of image is similar to the Joycean epiphany, as many critics pointed out, and, more generally, shows "confidence in syntheses gained through full exploitation of an everyday occurrence" in which "the totality of its fate is contained and can be portrayed" (Auerbach, 2003, p. 547; translation modified by the author). At the same time, the relevance of images and their paradigmatic value for the construction of a story (both in poetry and in prose) could also be related to the role of cinema in Pavese's imaginary (on which see Pavese 2009; Pietralunga 1991; Ferme 2001; Ventavoli 2010; an overview in Chirumbolo 2013). This interest has been linked to his idea of modernity, and to his understanding of the epitome of modern – the city – as well as to his choice of marginal characters (commons in American cinema of the Thirties) and for the temporal fragmentations, inspired perhaps by Chaplin's *Modern Times* (see Lorenzini 2009). Such role of cinema could be easily related to some of the American authors Pavese translated and avidly read: Dos Passos (Foster 1986; Pizer 2012; Schaefer 2019; Nanney 2020), Steinbeck, and Faulkner (Kawin 1977; Harrington and Abadie 1979; Solomon 2014). All these authors take from the popular movies of their years.

---

[7] This is strinkingly similar to Gadda's ideas: truth can be attained only through the work of art (Donnarumma 2006, 17).

[8] While rhetorical figures as metaphors used by post-symbolist Italian poets "have a mediating function between the speaker and his listeners, Pavese searches for an immediate adhesion to the object" (Imberty 2002, 8).

4. Structural features: rhythm, montage, dialogue

Later, Pavese will somehow reconsider the centrality of image-telling in his narrative, while still insisting on the exterior quality of his prose (and on the role of image: Ferraris 2002, 126). This comes together with the augmented importance of rhythm, which is seen as the way to let the sense emerge through short bursts of elements in the texture and not only as a prosodic concept. As Pavese wrote in his diary, he wants "(t)o suggest, by a repeated action, a descriptive name, some cross-reference or other, that a character, an object, or a situation in the story has an imaginative link with another". This "imaginative link" must "color" the whole work (Pavese 2017, 124).

Such a strategy implies strong ties among the vertical levels of the text. Pavese switched from a more superficial form of connection (i.e., the "exterior monologue" of his first works) to a deeper one. In this sense, Grasso's remarks on the continuous elaboration of isotopic webs during the revisions of his novels reveal the work on the material to let these "images" filtrate through the texture, and the scholar's observations are more relevant since she concentrates on the middle works of Pavese which, according to Guglielminetti, were written after the focus on the exterior monologue. For Sbrocchi, "rhythm is the keyword of Pavesian stylistics", and if this is true for all of his works, in the later phase, the rhythm reveals the symbolic elements, which emerges through brief elements of the texture (the "color") (Sbrocchi 1967, 85-6). These elements are externalized, too: they are the ones which "deal with reality *en bloc*, whose harsh experiences give rhythm, cadences, embellishments to his story" (Pavese 2017, 288; French and italics by Pavese). Externalized, but symbolical, as Pavese himself makes clear in his examples: Hemingway's has "violent death", Levi the "prison", Joyce "the stereoscope of words-sensations", Proust "the impossibility of seizing fleeting moments", Mann "the *mythical* reassessment of facts". Thus, the exterior level of the discourse could be fragmented into many loosely related scenes, but the plot is thematically tight due to the symbolic relationship between them (Isotti-Rosowsky 2000). Much as with Pavese's macrotexts, which determine the structure of the single text (Van den Bossche 2011).

While rhythm wraps up the work, other techniques, inspired by American writers, move in the opposite direction. Pavese prefers paratax and uses "vocal" narrators who seem to recount the story to someone (this debt is acknowledged by Pavese when talking of the "autobiography" of Faulkner's characters). He foregrounds the teller and the telling in a local context (as with the Faulknerian South, the Pavesian Langa, or alternatively the city, thanks to slang or vernacular language: Bozzola 1991; Laurenti 2011), thus rooting his judgments in the fictional world. This relativizes the interpretation, stressing the epistemological level of knowledge (such stress is archetypically Modernist:

McHale 1987). The same happens with the multiplication of perspectives, albeit this is more evident in Faulkner's or Anderson's use of multiple narrators, while Pavese usually focalizes on a single character – although the reader's role relativizes this, too (Isotti-Rosowski 2000).

Furthermore, Pavese multiplies the points of view through dialogues that allow characters to express their "absurd-ingenuous-mythical outpourings that cunningly interpret reality" (Pavese 2017, 65). The "exterior monologue" of his first novels served such strategy as well, but this became more evident with *Leucò* or also in many scenes of *La luna e i falò* with its extensive use of dialogues as a mean to clash interpretations (where the alternating montage also opposes two distinct perspectives, present vs. past).

Dialogues are now the way to show the relationship between subjectivities, and how they influence the events. This externalization highlights some elements of the psyche: not its constant change due to its fragmentation, but the way it determines the reactions to events. The fragmentation that arises from internal conflict between past and present (or memory and action) is only the starting point. In this sense, the freedom of his characters, also in *Leucò*, always stops before a Dostoevskijan "revolt of the character" (Bakhtin 1984, 26-27): the dialogic quality of his prose is always reduced. This is indeed the effect of the strict authorial control that Pavese deems important as the fundamental start of artistic creation: like in a domino, the author posits the pieces, then starts the game and lets things flow. One could relate this stance less to Naturalist *Romans experimentales* than to Italo Calvino's works, who was familiar with Pavese and who had similar ideas on artistic creation (see, for example, the "deductive short stories" in *Ti con zero*).

Moreover, the characters – rather than representing an ideologeme with their *words*, which would be a typical feature of Bakhtin's dialogism in the novel – are linked to their past and to what that past symbolizes through their *gestures*.[9] This past determines their moves, as it is the author who determines the background of characters: both block, limit, *severe* the freedom of characters. This is coherent with Pavese's idea that the modern novel shows a stable character: i.e., one that does not change.

This interest in dialogue, for the exteriorization of the self, detaches Pavese from other European Modernists, and again links him to American Modernism. The subjectivity is interesting for its *relational* value. Also, the U.S. contributed to his idea of myth, so different from those used by European Modernists such as Joyce or Mann (Lorenzi-Davitti 1975; Giobbi 1991). While in *Lavorare stanca* a Joyce-inspired Ulyssean under-text seemed to be at work (de las Nieves 1992,

---

[9] Note that in *Leucò* characters always discuss actions (usually, made by other people).

44), thus relating his poetry to that "mythical method" theorized by T.S. Eliot, later Pavese will consider the myth as a functional image or symbol for what the individual cannot change but must interpret: his own remote past, i.e., the childhood. It is well known that for Pavese, the "first time" was irrational, pre-logic, set apart from the (rational) knowledge, while it is only "the second time" that can establish a sense to the events (De Falco 2020; Guerbo 2020). Myth is used as a correlative objective to that inner experience which determines our later actions: a symbolic form of destiny. And, as Lanzillotta puts it, "the myth – the destiny – signals the fracture from the past: it determines the distance between yesterday and today", and the past determines the present; becoming aware of destiny helps to elaborate such persistence (Lanzillotta 2018, 372). In *this* sense Pavese re-elaborates the myth: it is not an actualization, a rewriting to bring out its essence, but the emersion of a symbolic problem – and its resolution. In this sense, the myth itself *is* transformed by its usage (Van den Bossche 2001).

5. Between Europe and the U.S.A: The Modernist Synthesis of Pavese

The connections between Modernism and Pavese were overlooked maybe because many scholars of Italian Modernists have a vision of Modernism carved on some elements: a strong stylistic innovation, albeit Pavese's style *is* surely innovative, but not in a direction of radical explosions of texts, especially at the linguistic and syntactic level (much more like Mann or Faulkner, than Joyce or Woolf); and the interest for the representation of subjectivity for itself, as a mean to show the multiple nature of the modern subject. Conversely, elements which appear as Neorealist (the interest for the ordinary situations, the lower-class characters, and the social themes) have somehow diverged the attention from other Modernist features, like a displaced/alienated subject, the role of psyche and perspectivism as a mean to disrupt the authorial narrator, the use of collage, the idea of "missed future" (Donnarumma 2006) emerging through the relationship between past and present, or the dichotomy city/countryside (which notably is not a feature typical of Italian Modernists, but common in other areas: Tortora 2018). It is true that some elements in Pavese are coherent with the new Italian literary panorama of the Thirties, but they are also typical of many Modernists, especially the American ones. This is particularly relevant if one looks at the sardonic stance Pavese took in the blurb of *Leucò* to those who considered him a "stubborn Neorealist". In this sense, it seems legitimate to ascribe those Neorealist features to the same social and exterior stance of American Modernists.

Part of the problem is perhaps a Eurocentric vision of Modernism. Although implicitly recognizing that other Modernisms can exist, many Italian scholars shape their concept on European Modernism (including here American expats), with only partial inclusions from the U.S., usually Faulkner and Dos Passos (the most stylistically coherent with European Modernism): a recent, thorough reading of Modernism outside Italy is devoted only to European Modernism (Tortora and Volpone 2018). This has also made more difficult to recognize certain authors as Modernists, like Sherwood Anderson, whose less experimental prose has been nonetheless recognized as fully Modernist (Bradbury 1983, 50). Anderson had an artistic trajectory strikingly similar to the one of Pavese: he, too, "was influenced by the vernacular of Mark Twain" while being "responsive to the prose experiments of Gertrude Stein" (Stouck 1985, 302).

Such a stance is certainly due to the fact that, until 1930s, American culture had a limited and difficult circulation in Italy; adding to this, the tendency of Italian criticists to consider the golden age of Modernism as ending with the twenties, makes clear why this latter part of Modernism had been overlooked in critical studies on Italian Modernism.

Although not extensively explored, there are some differences between European and American Modernisms, notably the role of mass media and culture. European Modernism has been conceptualized, after Adorno and Horkheimer, as a self-alienating form of art which tries to resist to the commodification of life. American Modernism, on the other hand, leans towards a less radical and negative use of mass culture, like the more nuanced one theorized by Walter Benjamin in many of his works like *The Work of Art* (1936).

Such leaning towards popular features typical of American modernism (Rabinowitz 2005) explains why its innovations are less extreme than its European counterpart: for example, Faulkner scholars recognize in his works a tension between an experimental and a representational impulse, and acknowledge the impulse on his narrative of "pure" storytelling (Bleikasten 1995), which goes with the role of commercial movies in his prose and plotting (Concolino 2008 reaches similar conclusions for Pavese). Cinema has a role also in structuring the novel, perhaps the place where both Pavese and his American models put the most of their innovative effort (for Dos Passos, see Wagner 1990, 28; Dow 1996).

Also, American modernists are keener to focus on the *social* aspect of life, which gives their works a flavor similar to Eighteenth-century books. As for his American models, the exteriority of Pavese's prose does not link directly to the Naturalist idea that the world could be known entirely through the visible and the sensible, but to the radical perspectivism of Modernist feature. As in Faulkner, Steinbeck (*Of Men and Mice*), or Anderson, the psychology is functional to the characters' comprehension of what is *happening* outside.

Thus, we can conclude that both for American modernists and Pavese the *thematic* (or topical) levels are like those of European modernists. What changes is the *rhematic* treatment, or the stylistic conversion of those principles – thus highlighting different elements in the texture. This is not to dilute the features of Modernism as a literary movement in a vaguer modernity: the deeper concerns are similar, and similar is the idea that art could symbolically (utopically) recompose the conflicts of the unfulfilled modernity, as Jameson (2002) wrote.

This feature is also typical of Pavese's works, and it strongly links him to Modernism: his effort to synthesize, and critically examine, the contrasting features of modernity.[10] Control and freedom (taking place at a narrative level in the tragic pattern of a destiny to fulfill and at authorial level where Pavese leaves characters free to act only inside an ordered frame) is a recurring dialectic in Pavese's work. Moreover, Lanzillotta (2012) observed that the oppositions at the base of Pavese's works (city-countryside; woman-man; childhood-adulthood; myth-history; rational-irrational) are not axiological dichotomies, as it is usually said, but in the textual configuration their nature is dialectical: antitheses which undergo a synthetic process. Each element of the couple is transformed by the other. Thus, the past of one's childhood as well as the myth (the "first time") is demystified by its revision in the present (and this changes the interpretation of both); the countryside is not better than the city, but they are mutually transformed. The rationality of the "second time" does not delete the irrational, original "first time", since the latter determines the former, but the former can better (i.e., rationally) understand the latter. This web of oppositions finds a synthesis in the use of symbols as a means to give a sense, which is not totally understandable through rationality, but can be rationally reconstructed by the reader (as he can reconstruct the parable of the main characters). This sense is obtained through architectural features (the "rhythm"), as well as through style — i.e., through form. As for all Modernists, the form of the work of art can still oppose some sort of coherence to modern world's fragmentation. But the concept of form is different: Pavese looks at the less disruptive forms of American Modernists, although his works resort to the very same strategies of all other Modernists: a synthesis that happens through vertical isotopies (i.e., the symbolic images that emerge through the rhythmic features). If we acknowledge that Modernism is a reaction to modernity in which the relationship between past and present, tradition and innovation, is dialectical and dynamic, it is logical that without clear manifestos and artistic groups, it is possible to find a variety of positions, all inside the same process of

---

[10] For Zaccaria, Pavese wanted to "locate and critically accept" modernity's "conflictual nodes" (Zaccaria 2001, 336).

negotiation between the two extremes, whose synthesis could vary. In such a frame, Pavese could be recognized as part of that movement, and the idea of Italian Modernism could be enriched by a new set of ideas and features.

Bibliography

Auerbach, E. (2003), *Mimesis. The Representation of Reality in Western Literature*. Princeton: Princeton University Press

Bakhtin, M. M. (1984). *Problems of Dostoevskij's Poetics*. Minneapolis: University of Minnesota Press

Baldi, V. (2010). *Reale invisibile. Mimesi e interiorità nella narrativa di Pirandello e Gadda*. Venezia: Marsilio

Bradbury, M. (1983). *The Modern American Novel*. Oxford: Oxford University Press

Comparini, A. (2017). *La poetica dei* Dialoghi con Leucò *di Cesare Pavese*. Sesto San Giovanni: Mimesis

Crocco, C. (2015). *La poesia italiana del Novecento*. Roma: Carocci

De Falco, A. (2020). "Dalla 'seconda volta' all''ultima battuta'", *Ticontre* (13), [Online]. Available at: https://doi.org/10.15168/t3.v0i13.415

de las Nieves Muñiz Muñiz, M. (1992). *Introduzione a Pavese*. Roma-Bari: Laterza

Domenichelli, M. (2005). *"Il grande schermo". Il mito americano in Italia fra gli anni Trenta e gli anni Cinquanta e* Il sentiero dei nidi di ragno *di Italo Calvino*, in Caltagirone, G. (ed). *La coscienza e il coraggio. Esperienze letterarie della modernità. Studi in onore di Sandro Maxia*. Cagliari: AM&D Edizioni, pp. 690-714

Donnarumma, R. (2006). *Gadda modernista*. Pisa: ETS

Eco, U. (1966). *Le poetiche di Joyce*. Milano: Bompiani

Ferme, V. (2002). *Tradurre è tradire: la traduzione come sovversione culturale sotto il Fascismo*. Ravenna: Longo

Ferraris, D. (2002). "Lo 'sguardo alla finestra' e il 'laborioso caos'. Sulla modernità narrativa di Pavese", *Narrativa*, 22, pp. 119-134

Fiedler, L. (1954). "Introducing Cesare Pavese", *Kenyon Review*, 4, pp. 536-553

Imberty, D. (2002). "Immagine-racconto e rapporti fantastici nell'opera di Cesare Pavese", *Narrativa*, 22, pp. 5-25

Isotti-Rosowski, G. (1988). "Cesare Pavese: dal naturalismo alla realtà simbolica", *Studi novecenteschi*, 15(36), pp. 273-321

Lanzillotta, M. (2018). *Uno sguardo sulla violenza: l'ultimo Pavese tra mito e storia*, in Alfano, G.; De Cristofaro, F. (eds.). *Il romanzo in Italia 3. Il primo Novecento*. Roma: Carocci, pp. 361-374

Mazzoni, G. (2011). *Teoria del romanzo*. Bologna: Il Mulino

Pavese, C. (1959). *The Comrade*, translated by W.J. Strachan. London: Peter Owen

———— (2017). *This Business of Living*. London: Routledge

———— (2021). *The Moon and the Bonfires*, translated by T. Parks. London: Penguin Books

Prieto, M. (1993). "La tradicion modernista", *Revista de lengua y literatura* 7, 13-14, pp. 61-66

Sbrocchi, L. (1967). *Stilistica nella narrativa pavesiana*. Frosinone: Casamari

Stouck, D. (1985). "Sherwood Anderson and the Postmodern Novel", *Contemporary Literature*, 26(3), pp. 302-316

Toracca, T. (2018). *Il neomodernismo italiano*, in Tortora, M. (ed.). *Il modernismo italiano*. Roma: Carocci, pp. 211-229

Wagner, L. (1990). *The Modern American Novel, 1914-1945: A Critical History*. Boston: Twayne

Zaccaria, G. (2001). *Pavese recensore e la letteratura americana (con alcuni testi dimenticati)*, in *Sotto il gelo dell'acqua c'è l'erba*. Alessandria: Edizioni dell'Orso, pp. 328-347

Further Reading

Bertoni, F. (2018). *Il modernismo internazionale e il rinnovamento delle tecniche in Italia*, in Alfano, G.; De Cristofaro, F. (eds.). *Il romanzo in Italia 3. Il primo Novecento*. Roma: Carocci, pp. 39-53

Billiani, F. (2019). "Le traduzioni pavesiane di Gertrude Stein: la scrittura come consapevolezza", *The italianist* (19), pp. 193-227

Bleikasten, A. (1995). *Faulkner from a European Perspective*, in Weinstein, P. M. (ed.). *The Cambridge Companion to William Faulkner*. Cambridge: Cambridge University Press, pp. 75-95

Bozzola, S. (1991). "Note su Pavese e Vittorini traduttori di Steinbeck", *Studi novecenteschi*, 18(41), pp. 63-101

Brooks, P. (1976). *The melodramatic imagination. Balzac, Henry James, Melodrama and the Mode of Excess*. New Haven: Yale University Press

Cangiano, D. (2018). *La nascita del modernismo italiano. Filosofie della crisi, storia e letteratura (1903-1922)*. Macerata: Quodlibet

Castellana, R. (2010). "Realismo modernista. Un'idea del romanzo italiano (1915-1925)", *Italianistica* 39(1), pp. 24-44

Chirumbolo, P. (2013). *Pavese e il cinema: lo stato attuale della critica*, in Catalfamo, A. (ed.). *Cesare Pavese: il mito classico e i miti moderni*. Catania: CUECM, pp. 97-108

Concolino, C. (2008). "Cesare Pavese and Film Noir. A Case of Convergent Sensibilities", *NeMLA Italian Studies*, 33, pp. 25-43

de las Nieves Muñiz Muñiz, M. (2001). *Tutti i romanzi*. Torino: Einaudi-Gallimard.

Dow, W. (1996). "John Dos Passos, Blaise Cendrars, and the 'Other' Modernism", *Twentieth Century Literature*, 42(3), pp. 396-415

Ferme, V. (2001). *Il giovane Pavese e il cinema americano*, in *Sotto il gelo dell'acqua c'è l'erba. Omaggio a Cesare Pavese*. Alessandria: Edizioni dell'Orso, pp. 15-40

Foster, G. (1986). "John Dos Passos' Use of Film Technique in *Manhattan Transfer* and *The 42nd Parallel*", *Literature/Film Quarterly*, 14 (3), pp. 186-194

Giobbi, G. (1991). "Pavese and Joyce: Exile, Myth, and the Past", *Journal of European Studies*, 21, pp. 43-53

Grasso, M. (2020). "Un'umanità alle soglie della coscienza", *Ticontre* (13), [Online]. Available at: https://doi.org/10.15168/t3.v0i13.408

Guglielminetti, M. (2001). *Cesare Pavese romanziere*, in Pavese, C. *Tutti i romanzi*. Torino: Einaudi-Gallimard, pp. ix-lxvi

Harrington, E. and Abadie, A. J. (eds.). (1979). *Faulkner, Modernism, and Film*. Jackson: U of Mississippi Press

Huyssen, A. (1986). *After the Great Divide: Modernism, Mass Culture, Postmodernism*. Bloomington: Indiana University Press

Isotti-Rosowski, G. (2000). "Pavese: il romanzo deludente", *Esperienze letterarie*, 25(3-4), pp. 87-101

Jameson, F. (2002). *A Singular Modernity. Essay on the Ontology of Present*. London: Verso

Kavaloski, J. (2014). *High Modernism: Aestheticism and Performativity in Literature of the 1920s*. Rochester (NY): Camden House

Kawin, B.F. (1977). *Faulkner and Film*. New York: Ungar

King, M. (1972). "Cesare Pavese: Reluctant Translator of James Joyce", *James Joyce Quarterly*, 9(3), pp. 374-382

Kokubo, M. (2017). "La poetica modernista di Cesare Pavese in *Lavorare stanca*", *Poetiche*, 19(47), pp. 283-308

Lanzillotta, M. (2012). *Città in campagna e campagna in città nella poesia di Cesare Pavese*, in Barenghi, M.; Langella, G.; Turchetta, G. (eds.). *La città e l'esperienza del moderno*. Pisa: ETS, pp. 461-471

Laurenti, F. (2011). "Pavese e la scoperta dei dialetti italiani attraverso la traduzione degli americani", *Studi novecenteschi*, 38 (82), pp. 329-337

Lorenzi-Davitti, P. (1975). *Pavese e la cultura americana. Tra mito e razionalità*. Firenze-Messina: D'Anna

Lorenzini, N. (2009). "Lavoro, città, spaesamento: sul set di *Lavorare stanca*", *Letteraria*, 2, pp. 101-106

Luperini, R.; Tortora, M. (eds.). (2012). *Sul modernismo italiano*. Napoli: Liguori

Mao, D.; Walkowitz, R. (2009). "The New Modernist Studies", *PMLA*, 123(3), pp. 737-748

McHale, B. (1987). *Postmodernist Fiction*. London: Routledge

Meneghelli, D. (2013). "Periodization, Comparative Literature, and Italian Modernism", *CLCWeb: Comparative Literature and Culture*, 15(7), [Online]. Available at: https://doi.org/10.7771/1481-4374.2386

Milani, M. (2009). "Pavese & Joyce: monologhi interiori e 'immagini-racconto'", *Poetiche*, 1, pp. 39-61

Moretti, F. (1987). *Segni e stili del moderno*. Torino: Einaudi

———— (2003). *Opere-mondo* Torino: Einaudi

Nanney, L. (2020). *John Dos Passos & Cinema*. Liverpool: Liverpool University Press

Pavese, C. (1968). *Saggi letterari*. Torino: Einaudi

———— (2009). *Il serpente e la colomba. Scritti e soggetti cinematografici*. Torino: Einaudi

Pellini, P. (2016). *Naturalismo e modernismo. Zola, Verga e la poetica dell' insignificante*. Roma: Artemide

Pietralunga, M. (1991). "The Young Pavese's Thoughts on Cinema", *Romance Languages Annual*, 3, pp. 299-302

—— (2005). *Il mito di una scoperta: Pavese traduce* Passage to India *di Walt Whitman*, in Campanello, M. (ed.). *Cesare Pavese: atti del convegno internazionale di studi*. Firenze: Olschki, pp. 111-130

Pizer, D. (2012). "John Dos Passos in the 1920s: The Development of a Modernist Style", *Mosaic: An Interdisciplinary Critical Journal*, 45(4), pp. 51-67

Pomilio, T. (2019). "Engagement e stilizzazione. L'effetto Hemingway negli italiani a cavallo della Seconda Grande Guerra", *'900 transnazionale*, 3(1), [Online]. Available at: https://doi/10.13133/2532-1994_3.3_2019

Rabinowitz, P. (2005). *Social representations within American modernism*, in Kalaidjian, W. (ed.). *The Cambridge Companion to American Modernism*. Cambridge: Cambridge University Press, pp. 261-283

Riccobono R. (2018). *Cesare Pavese e la crisi del narratore moderno*, in Somigli, L.; Conti, E. (eds.). *Oltre il canone: problemi, autori, opere del modernismo italiano*. Perugia: Morlacchi, pp. 191-205

Rogers, G. (2014). "Jiménez, Modernism/o, and the Languages of Comparative Modernist Studies", *Comparative Literature*, 66(1), pp. 127-147

Rubeo, U. (2019). "Una lezione di antiretorica: Hemingway e gli scrittori italiani", *'900 transnazionale*, 3(1), [Online]. Available at: https://doi.org/10.13133/2532-1994_3.1_2019

Schaefer, H. (2019). *"A Novel Like a Documentary Film": Cinematic Writing as Cultural Critique in John Dos Passos's* Manhattan Transfer, in Schaefer, H. *American Literature and Immediacy: Literary Innovation and the Emergence of Photography, Film, and Television*. Cambridge: Cambridge University Press, pp. 143-170

Shaw, D. L. (2002). "When Was Modernism in Spanish-American Fiction?", *Bulletin of Spanish Studies*, 79(2-3), pp. 395-409

Sichera, A. (2000). "Pavese nei dintorni di Joyce. Le 'due stagioni' del *Carcere*", *Esperienze letterarie*, 3-4, pp. 121-152

Solomon, S. (2014). *Faulkner and the Masses: A Hollywood Fable*, in Lurie, P. and Abadie, A. J. (eds.). *Faulkner and Film*. Jackson: U of Mississippi Press, pp. 98-118

Somigli, L.; Moroni, M. (2004). *Italian Modernism: Italian Culture between Decadentism and Avant-Garde*. Toronto: University of Toronto Press

Stein, T. (2007). "'Caccia', 'pesca' e 'guerra'. Pavese lettore di Hemingway da *Primo amore* a *La luna e i falò*", *Rassegna europea della letteratura italiana*, 15, pp. 137-157

Tortora, M. (2010). *Debenedetti, Svevo e il modernismo*, in Cataldi, P. (ed.) *Per Romano Luperini*. Palermo: Palumbo, pp. 281-302

—— (2018a). *Città e campagna*, in Alfano, G. and De Cristofaro, F. (eds.). *Il romanzo in Italia 3. Il primo Novecento*. Roma: Carocci, pp. 233-252

—— (ed.). (2018b). *Il modernismo italiano*. Roma: Carocci

Tortora, M. and Volpone, A. (eds.). (2018). *Il romanzo modernista europeo*. Roma: Carocci

Van den Bossche, B. (2001). *Nulla è veramente accaduto. Strategie discorsive del mito nell'opera di Cesare Pavese.* Firenze-Leuven: Cesati-Leuven University Press

———— (2011). *Pavese e il macrotesto:* Lavorare stanca, Feria d'agosto, Dialoghi con Leucò, in Concolino, C. (ed.). *Cesare Pavese a San Francisco.* Firenze: Cesati: 115-125

Ventavoli, L. (2010). *Visioni. Possibili itinerari cinematografici di Cesare Pavese.* Torino: NIP

Ziolkowski, S.E. (2020). *Kafka's Italian Progeny.* Toronto: Toronto University Press

Contributors

Antonio Garrasi currently holds a clarinet position with the Civic Orchestra of Chicago and collaborates regularly with the Chicago Symphony Orchestra. He briefly attended the University of Catania, studying Foreign Languages and Literatures, before dedicating himself to music, but never abandoned his passion for the written arts. Upon completing his bachelor's degree, Antonio moved to the United States, graduating with his Professional Diploma in Orchestral Studies from Roosevelt University (Chicago) in 2018. Then, in 2020, he graduated with a Master of Arts in Music Performance from Northwestern University (Chicago) and continued his education at Northwestern University with a post-baccalaureate in Pre-Medicine. He has recently submitted a medical case report, Arthroscopic Excision of the Pigmented Villonodular Synovitis (PVNS) of the Trochanteric Bursitis of the Hip, which has been approved for publication in the Sports Medicine Journal – Orthopedics.

Carlo Tirinanzi De Medici is fixed-term researcher in Literary Criticism and Comparative Literature at Pisa University. He has worked at Brown University, Malta University, Trento University, Turin University and at Venice-based Fondazione Cini. He is co-director of journal "Ticontre. Teoria Testo Traduzione" and of the poetry series "Gli Albatri", and takes part to the SEMPER - Seminario permanente di poesia and SIT - Seminario d'interpretazione testuale. He wrote a book on realism in contemporary Western novels (*Il vero e il convenzionale*, 2012) and one on Italian novels of the last 40 years (*Il romanzo italiano contemporaneo. Dalla fine degli anni Settanta a oggi*, 2018, third-place at the Edinburgh Gadda Prize).

Francesco Chianese is Marie Skłodowska-Curie Research Fellow (2020-23) at Cardiff University and California State University, Long Beach. At CSULB, he was also a Fulbright Scholar-in-Residence (2018-19) and taught Italian and Italian American culture. He was awarded a John F. Kennedy Institute Library Grant (2019), a DAAD Short Research Grant (2015), and an EAAS Travel Grant (2014), all spent at the John F. Kennedy Institute, Freie Universität, Berlin. In 2018, he published the book *"Mio padre si sta facendo un individuo problematico": Padri e figli nell'ultimo Pasolini (1966-75)*. His articles and essays have been published in the journals "Women Language Literature in Italy / Donne Lingua Letteratura in Italia" (2022), "Translation and Interpreting Studies" (2022), "Diacritica" (2022), "Ticontre" (2020), "Italian Studies" (2018), "Between" (2015, 2016), and "Iperstoria" (2015), as well as in the volumes *La* *lezione di Pasolini* (2020), *Italian Americans on Screen* (2020) and *Harbors, Flows and Migrations: The USA in/and the World* (2017).

Iuri Moscardi is a PhD Candidate in Comparative Literature at the Graduate Center of the City University di New York, and teaches Italian language and literature at Hunter College and Fordham University. He studied Cesare Pavese at the University of Milan: his Bachelor's degree thesis focused on the end of the American myth in *The Moon and the Bonfires* and his Master's degree thesis, awarded with Premio Pavese, proved the participation of Pavese in Pivano's first Italian translation of *Spoon River Anthology*. In 2016 he received a MA in Italian from Indiana University, Bloomington. His dissertation focuses on Italian authors (among which Pavese), Digital Humanities, and the reception theory. He has published articles and essays on Pavese, in Italian and English, and edited the new, complete English translation of Pavese's diary. He collaborates with Fondazione Pavese: he is studying the books donated by the Molina family to Fondazione Pavese.

Kim Grego is Associate Professor of English Language and Translation at the University of Milan, where she teaches English Language and Linguistics. Her interests include Translation Studies, ESP (scientific, medical and political discourse), Critical Genre Analysis and Critical Discourse Studies applied to ethically debatable issues.

Maria Concetta Trovato currently collaborates with the University of Catania as a subject expert in Italian contemporary literature and works as a tenured teacher of Literary Disciplines in Modica (Ragusa). In 2012, after graduating with honors in Foreign Languages and Literatures at the University of Catania, she started a PhD in Modern Philology: her research project consisted of a critical edition of Cesare Pavese's *Dialoghi con Leucò* (*Dialogues with Leucò*) and is currently under publication. In 2014 and in 2016 she was awarded the Pavese Giovani Prize for two essays, the first of which exploring the echoes of Dante in Pavese's literary works. In 2018, she graduated for the second time in Modern Philology and in 2021 she contributed to the publication of Cesare Pavese's complete poetic oeuvre (*L'opera poetica,* Mondadori, 2021).

Mark Pietralunga is a professor of Italian Studies and former chair of the Department of Modern Languages and Linguistics at Florida State University (Tallahassee, Florida). He has a degree in English literature from UCLA and a Ph.D. in Italian literature from the University of California, Berkeley. He has published various books and numerous articles on Italian literature and culture of the 20th century and Italian American literature and culture. His books include *Beppe Fenoglio and English Literature: A Study of the Writer as Translator*

(University of California Press 1987); *Prometeo slegato: Pavese traduttore di P. B. Shelley* (Einaudi 1997); *Beppe Fenoglio: Quaderno di Traduzioni* (Einaudi, 2000); *Cesare Pavese and Anthony Chiuminatto: Their Correspondence* (University of Toronto Press 2007); *Cesare Pavese's Long Journey: A Critical-Analytical Study by Giose Rimanelli* (Bordighera Press, 2019), and *Italians in America by Amerigo Ruggiero* (Bordighera Press, 2020).

Monica Lanzillotta is Associate Professor of Contemporary Italian Literature at the Department of Culture, Education and Society of the University of Calabria. Her research interest lies in different areas of investigation: the persistence of the classical tradition in twentieth-century Italy, fantastic literature, theatre literature, the relationship between literature and music and between literature and medicine. He has published numerous articles and books on Pavese, including the most recent: *Cesare Pavese una vita tra Dioniso e Edipo*, published by Carocci in 2022.

Salvatore Renna studied Classical Philology at the University of Turin (B.A., M.A.). He received a PhD in Comparative Literature from the University of Bologna and L'Aquila and he has been a Post-Doc Researcher at the Freie Universität in Berlin. He has published, with Enrico Mattioda, a new edition of Cesare Pavese's *Mestiere di vivere* (BUR 2021) and, among the others, he has published articles about Philip Roth, Cormac McCarthy, and Pier Vittorio Tondelli. His research interests include modern and contemporary reception of classical culture, literary theory, and the relationship between city and literary expression.

Index

Y

www.ingramcontent.com/pod-product-compliance
Lightning Source LLC
Chambersburg PA
CBHW050529270326
41926CB00015B/3135